UNIFORMS OF THE SOVIET UNION

UNIFORMS OF THE SOVIET UNION

1918-1945

David Webster
& Chris Nelson

Schiffer Military History
Atglen, PA

Acknowledgments

This work is the result of collection and research by David Webster and Chris Nelson with photography by Robert Biondi. The authors wish to thank the following individuals for their contributions and support: Yuri Altshuler, Doug Drabik, Jim Gavigan, Alex Grossman, Phil Hirakas, Les Kirby, Wayne Krug, Al Lenartson, Jim MacDonald, Kevin Mahoney, Igor Moiseyev, Andrew Scoulas, Ilia Shapiro, Larry Stewart, Greg Stone, Serguei Tsapenko, Richard Washington, Dave Williams, and Sue Webster. Thanks also to Bruce Camburn and the staff of Graphic Imaging Services for their superb work.

If you would like to correspond with the authors about the book contact: Dave Webster, P.O. Box 423, Albion, MI 49224.

Dedication

This work is dedicated to Sue Webster who has given the author countless hours of her time, counseling, editing, typing, and proof reading. Without her organizational skills and gentle prodding this book would have taken far longer to complete.

Photography and book design by Robert Biondi.

Library of Congress Catalog Number: 98-84261.

Printed in China.
ISBN: 0-7643-0527-1

We are interested in hearing from authors with book ideas on related topics.

Published by Schiffer Publishing Ltd.
4880 Lower Valley Road
Atglen, PA 19310 USA
Phone: (610) 593-1777
FAX: (610) 593-2002
E-mail: Schifferbk@aol.com.
Please write for a free catalog.
This book may be purchased from the publisher.
Please include $3.95 postage.
Try your bookstore first.

Contents

Introduction

This book is a combination of visual and descriptive information about military uniforms and insignia of the Soviet Union from 1918 through 1945. Interest in regalia of this period has been broadened due to recent political changes in the former Soviet Union. Hundreds of full color highly detailed photographs of actual artifacts are in this book. In addition, many black and white period photographs are published here for the first time. Uniforms from the rank of Marshal of the Soviet Union to the private soldier of all service arms are to be found in this extensive volume.

The book begins with the revolutionary period, and continues through the civil war, the rebuilding period of the 1920s, and the beginnings of the modern Soviet military of the early 1930s, including the restoration of military ranks. From 1935 to 1943 the Soviet Union saw enhancements of various corps within the military with the new uniforms of 1940 emulating other militaristic nations of the time. In 1943 the reintroduction of Imperial insignia and uniforms, suppressed for so long by the Bolsheviks and Soviet military, was initiated. This change of concept during the war to defeat the Fascist invaders was considered patriotic in the traditional sense.

CHAPTER ONE

1918-1935

In 1917 the factions involved in the revolution were using Imperial Russian Uniforms. Modifications were made to those uniforms so the revolutionaries could recognize their comrades. A piece of red fabric tied around the left arm was the first insignia used by the Bolsheviks. Red fabric was also used to modify headgear and all Imperial insignia was removed from the uniforms.

Within a few months the Bolsheviks were introducing insignia and new uniform regulations. The most striking of these was the pointed winter cap with side flaps and large star on the front. Rank insignia made its appearance on sleeves within a bracketed area above the cuff. At this time the Bolsheviks were attempting to impose a system of equality: a classless system in the military. To the untrained eye, the difference between common soldier and high ranking official was difficult to discern. The use of colored triangles, squares or diamonds comprised the levels of command. Titles of General, officer, or sergeant were not used.

During the latter part of the 1920s plain and simple uniforms were introduced. The basic color was brown (or dark blue for Air Force) with black buttons. This plain look with color only in the cap star and collar tabs was regulation until 1935.

Names of the uniformed security forces changed over the years. The first internal security police of the state was the Cheka. After restructuring it was the GPU; later the Unified State Political Department or OGPU. In 1934 a new name was adopted and used through the war: Peoples Commissariats for Internal Affairs, more commonly known as the NKVD. Also existing at this time was the Central Directorate of State Security or GUGB. This became the overseeing organization for all security forces in the USSR.

Early Red Army uniforms were Czarist leftovers worn with newly approved rank insignia. This example still has holes in the shoulders where Czarist shoulder boards had been attached.

Summer service dress for Red Commander, circa 1920.

Red Guard units often wore a red arm band.

Lower Sleeve insignia of Artillery with four squares indicates Artillery Regiment Commander.

GPU Railway Security Agent 1922. The uniform is made of a coarse black wool with black velvet collar tabs piped in red. The GPU or State Political Administration grew out of the reorganized Cheka in February 1922.

Collar tabs indicate GPU. Detail of new buttons show hammer and sickle instead of formerly used hammer and plow.

A single Red Star with red piping was regulation in 1922. No additional insignia under the star indicates the lower rank of agent.

Cavalry Gymnastiorka 1919. This visor cap is named to the 8th Division, 44th Regiment. Cavalry units wore distinctive visor cap color combinations.

Sleeve insignia denoting branch of service were introduced in 1920. This distinctive horse head patch is worn by cavalry. This is the first pattern patch.

1919 pattern Cavalry gymnastiorka has collar tabs in addition to breast tabs.

This horseshoe patch is the third pattern Cavalry patch used before 1924 uniform revisions.

Revolutionary Troops 1918.

Many troops are mounted personnel 1924.

Model 1919 Gymnastiorka worn by infantry assistant platoon leader. Brick red insignia is GPU troops.

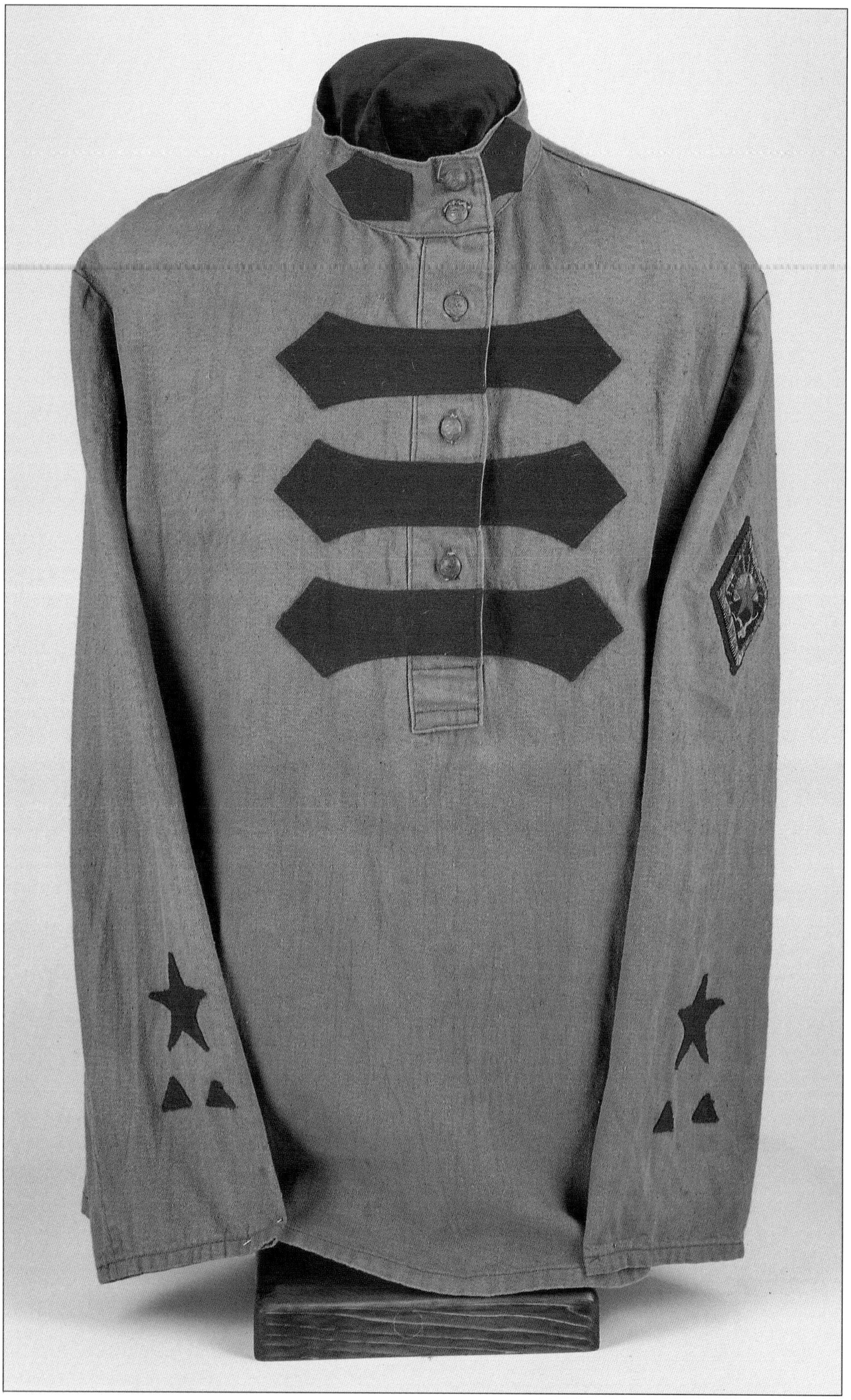

Buttons have hammer and plow in raised relief.

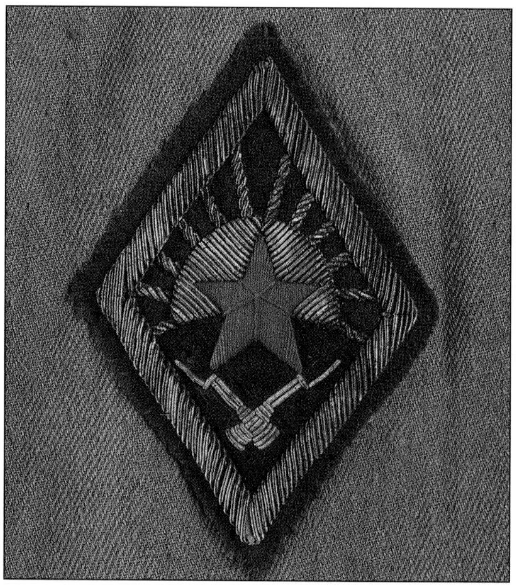

Sleeve patch is same as regular infantry except backing is brick red.

Right: The star and triangles are the same color and material as the breast tabs. January 1919 regulation prescribed that rank insignia be sewn directly to the sleeve. Later they were sewn to a sleeve patch.

Collar insignia indicate the district where the officer served.

In January 1922 new rank insignia were sewn to a sleeve patch rather than directly to the sleeve. The patch matched branch of service colors on collar tabs and breast patches.

Stamped on the linen lining of the front pocket is the acceptance stamp dating the uniform 1922.

This Gymnastiorka of 1922 with forest green insignia piped in red indicates Regimental Commander of Administrative Troops. The slit pocket was regulation in 1924, but was later eliminated.

Air Force summer Gymnastiorka Model 1919 with 1922 insignia.

Air Force arm patch.

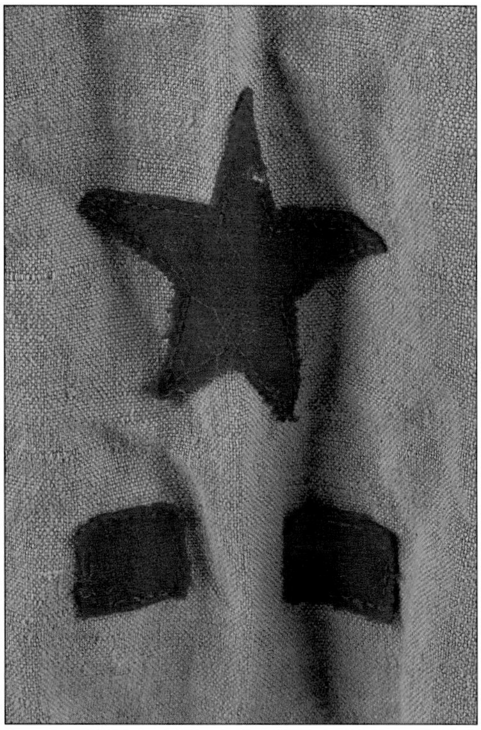

Two squares below the star on the lower sleeve indicate the rank of Company Commander. These are sewn to the sleeve per 1919 regulation.

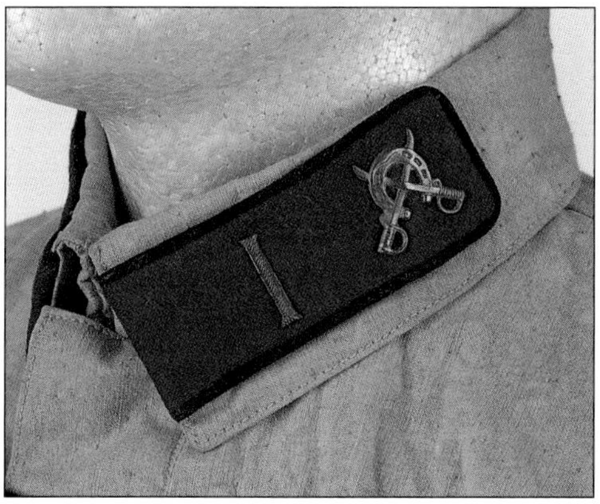

Branch of service insignia on collar tabs came into use January 31, 1922 when collar tabs were enlarged and piped.

A less elaborate Cavalry upper sleeve insignia was introduced in April 1920.

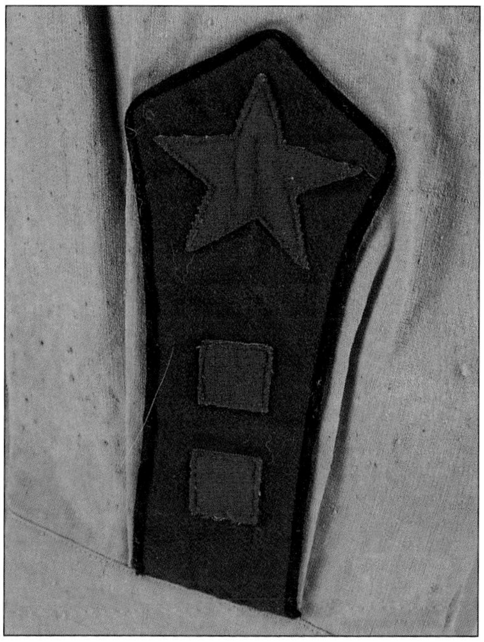

The lower sleeve patch indicates the rank of Company Commander. The only difference between an officer and an enlisted mans uniform was the insignia below the star on the lower sleeve.

Right: Date stamp on inside of Gymnastiorka. This example was manufactured in 1923.

Cavalry summer uniform Model 1919 with 1922 regulation sleeve patches.

Right: Officers at break 1925.

Senior Commander 1924.

Right: Troops in the field, 1924.

Infantry private Gymnastiorka Model 1919 with the 1922 sleeve patch.

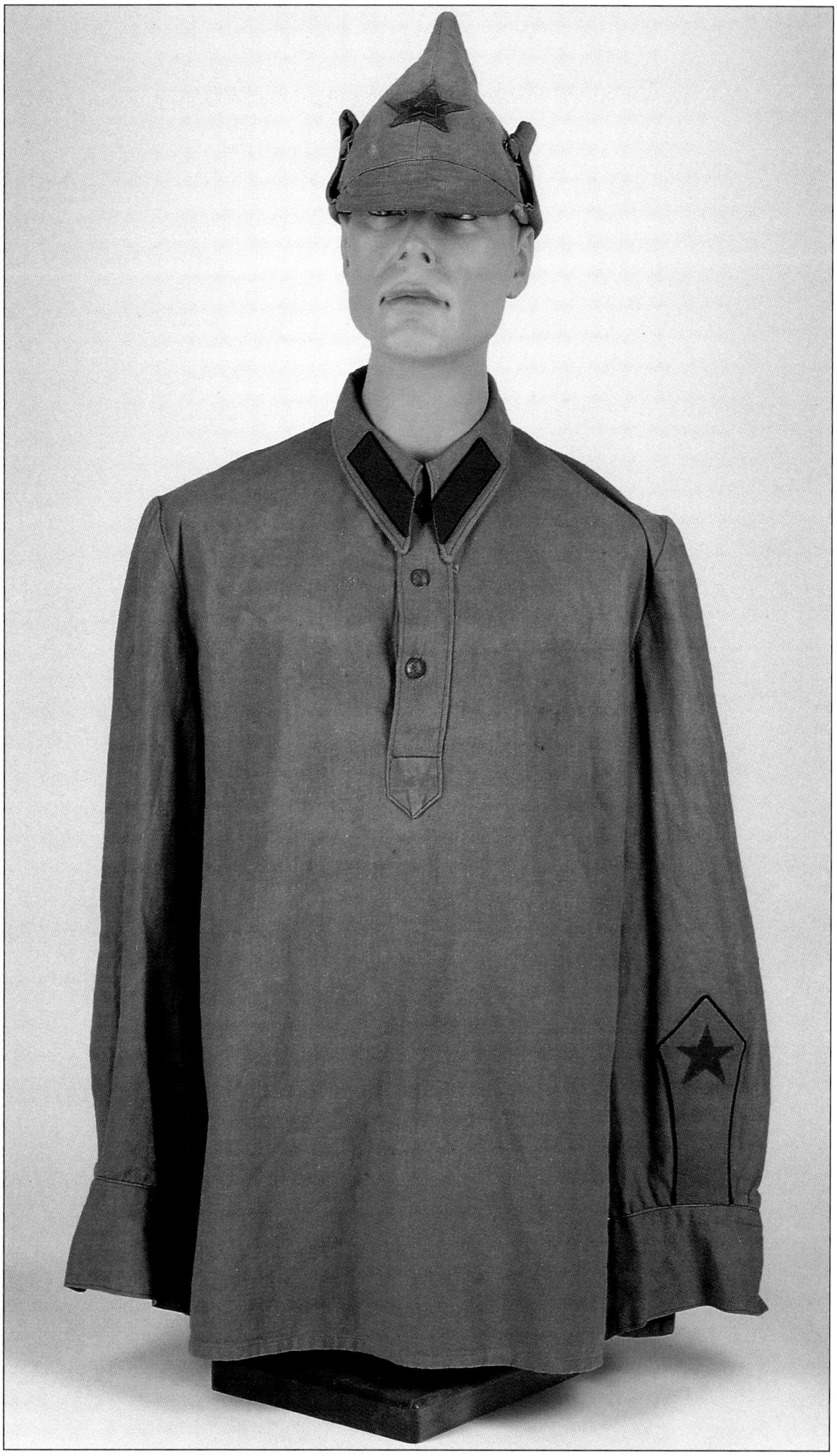

This colorful greatcoat, called a kaftan, was introduced in 1919. The color combination of crimson with the green piped black star is associated with General Staff officials.

Detail of black star piped with green on a crimson field on lower sleeve of greatcoat.

Cavalry Brigade Commander tunic used between 1922 and 1927.

Cavalry insignia mounted on plain tab. *(Photos this page by Les Kirby)*

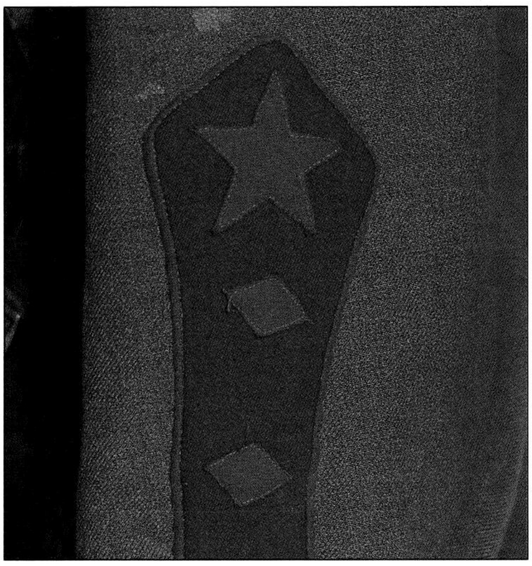

The enamel diamonds denote the highest level of rank for this period.

GPU prisoner transport soldier's summer Gymnastiorka. This uniform conforms to 1919 regulation, updated in 1922 to include collar devices.

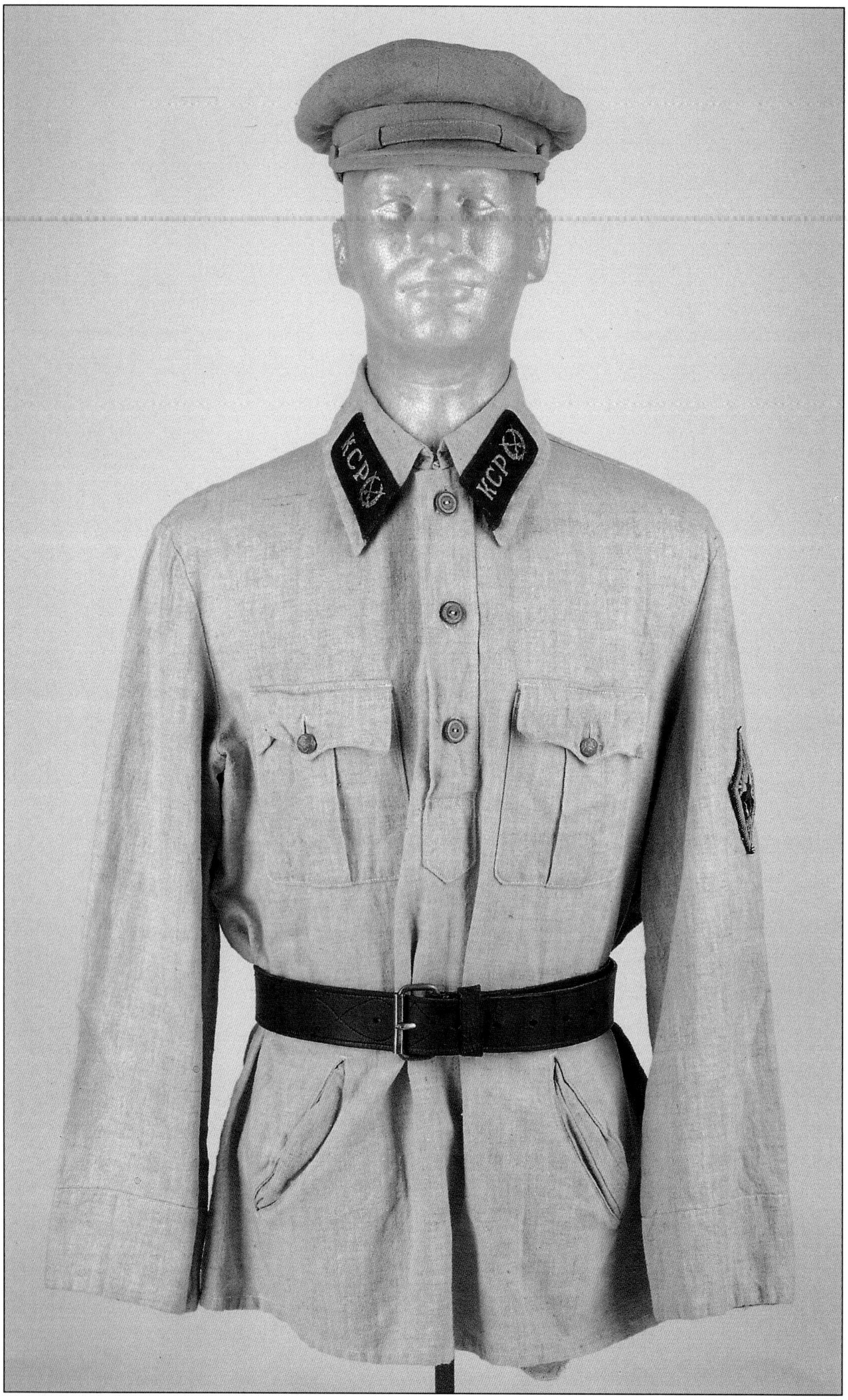

Details of the GPU collar insignia.

Upper sleeve insignia with sword and rifle indicates transportation troops.

Medium Commander, 1927.

Senior Commander, 1926.

The 1924, the uniform changed to a jacket with two button pockets on the chest and two slit pockets on the skirt. The five buttons are blued steel. The visor cap changed to a flatter visor and a shorter rise.

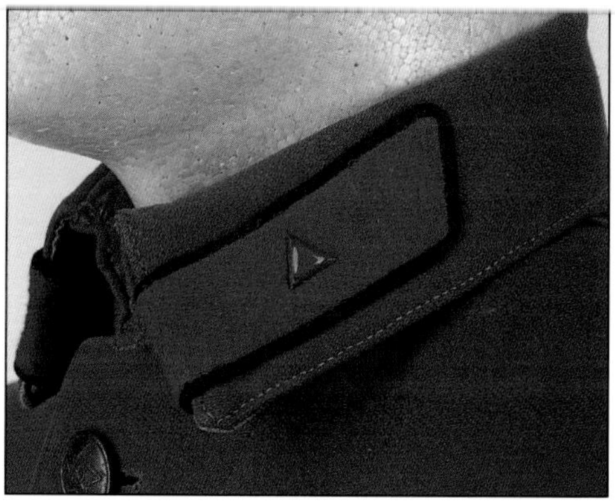

Collar insignia with one triangle are worn by infantry section commander. This is the next rank above private.

OGPU Private,1924. When the Soviet Union was formed in 1923 the GPU was renamed OGPU (Unified State Political Organization). The insignia is the only indicator of branch of service.

OGPU retained the red branch color from the GPU.

Platoon Commander of Engineers Model 1924. This uniform has four pleated pockets in the style reserved for commanders.

Black collar tabs with one square for rank and the shovel and pickax insignia for Engineers. Buttons are the blued steel.

Air Force Academy cadet Model 1924. The tunic is the same five-button style as regular army troops.

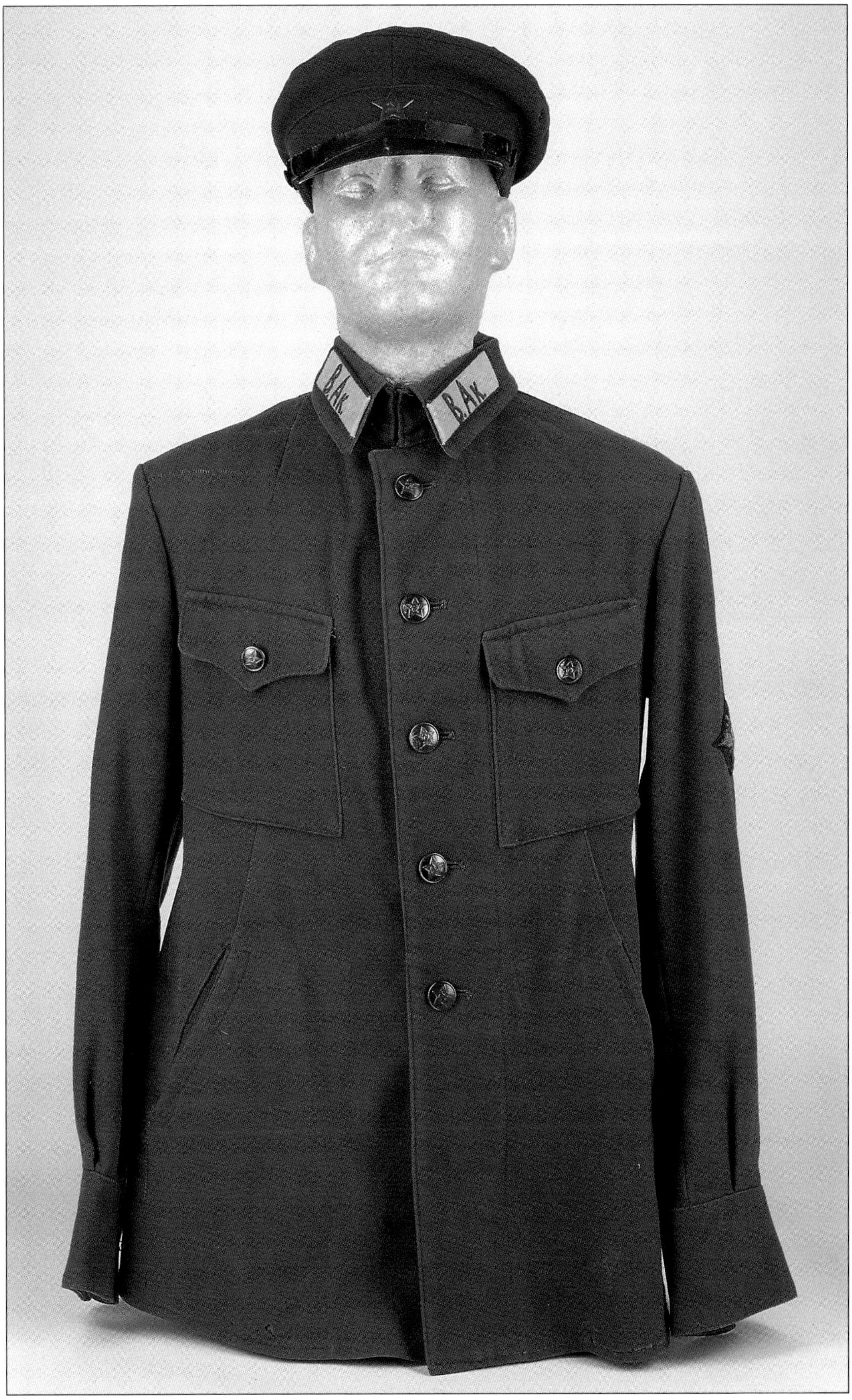

Light blue collar tabs represent Air Force with the Academy designation in gold.

Detail of new pilot sleeve insignia. The pilots wore crossed swords and wings.

Red Guard detachment 1924.

Air Force Senior rank, medium command personnel, circa 1933.

Gymnastiorka Summer 1924. This tunic has neither the covered buttons nor pleated pockets that were regulation at the time.

Details of Infantry Private Model 1924 collar tabs.

Right: These soldiers are wearing a greatcoat in use from 1918 through 1942. The coat was closed with hooks rather than buttons, circa 1934.

Above: Same soldiers as in portrait below right. Note Leader and Ranks belt.

Right: 4th Rank of Medium Command Personnel and Private Armor branch.

OGPU Official, 1920s.

Collar tabs indicate district and group.

OGPU Official summer service, circa 1934.

OGPU Official attached to a Rifles Formation, circa 1934

Right: Senior Commander 1933.

Below: Senior Commanders, one is Armor another is Colonel of Air Force and the last two are Infantry. Circa 1934.

NKVD Official, State Security.

New pattern of collar tab with narrower angled end, circa 1935.

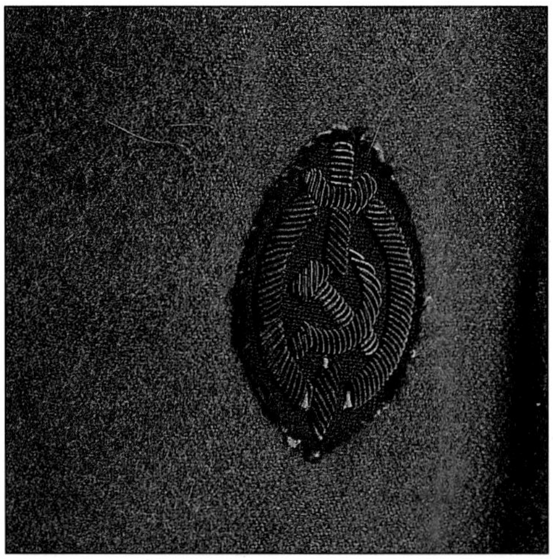

Sleeve insignia adopted in 1934.

Left: Model 1919 winter issue soft helmet was originally called a bogatyrka or a schlem. The 1st Cavalry Division wore the newly issued helmet and renamed it budenovka in honor of Commander Budenny. The high peak emulated the spike on a Russian knight's helmet of the 13th century. It served to distinguish Bolshevik troops from the enemy, even at a distance. Uniforms of the Reds and Whites prior to 1919 were drawn primarily from surplus Czarist stock so the new helmet was issued to prevent infiltration by the enemy. Cap insignia is a crossed hammer and plow, representing the union of rural and urban workers. Right: Brushed cotton budenovka with a black artillery star. This example has hammer and plow brass buttons instead of the usual cloth covered buttons.

Cavalry Model 1918.

Summer weight soft helmet made of corduroy Model 1919.

Red leather budenovka attributed to crewmen on Trotsky's armored trains.

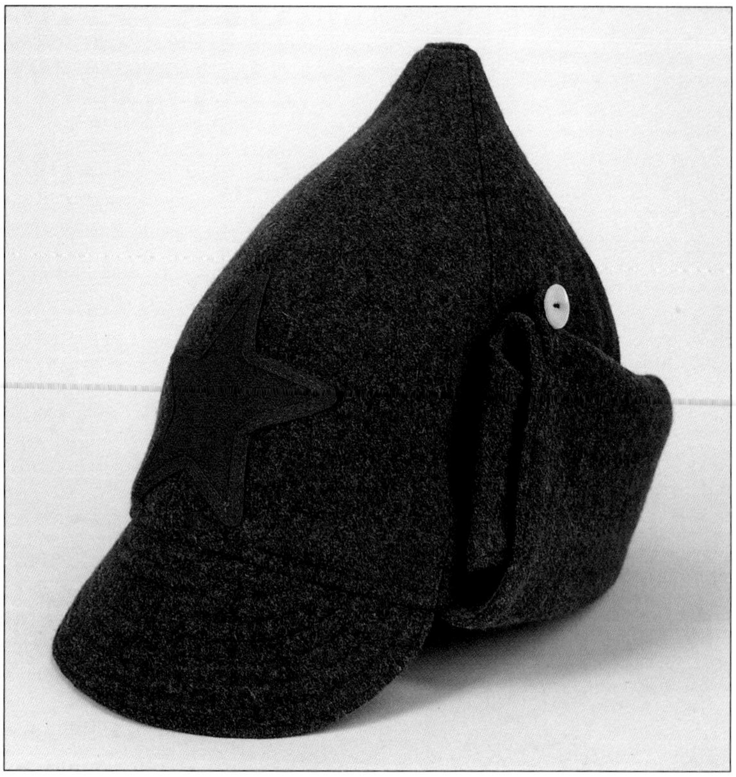

OGPU/NKVD, circa 1927.

OGPU Railroad Security budenovka.

Artillery budenovka without the usual pointed peak. The style was distinctive to artillery schools.

Cavalry Summer weight budenovka made of canvas with a visor in front and back.

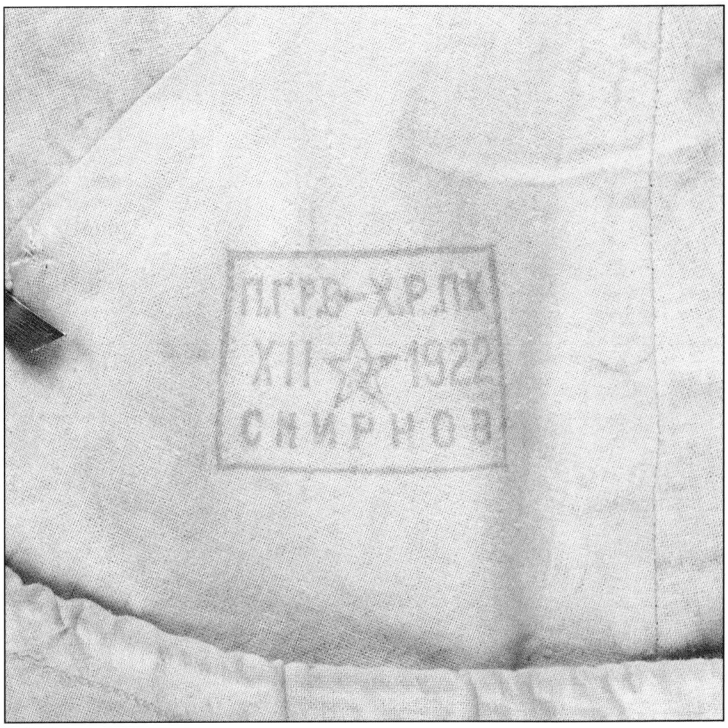

Stamp marking on linen lining of a summer budenovka indicates 1922 manufacture.

Imperial Air Force Pilotka was converted to Soviet use by adding a red star.

Visor Cap, Eighth Cavalry Division, 44th Regiment Model 1919. Cap cover is red with black piping and light blue band. The red painted star is cut from sheet steel and impressed with the hammer and sickle.

OGPU Railway Security Agent visor cap.

Right: Visor cap for State Security. These colors served the GPU, OGPU and NKVD.

Militia Visor Cap Model 1919. Right: Inside of Militia Visor Cap Model 1919 showing manufacturers label.

Field visor cap constructed of dark green wool with a light green visor. The star is a thick cast metal lightly pebbled to retain paint.

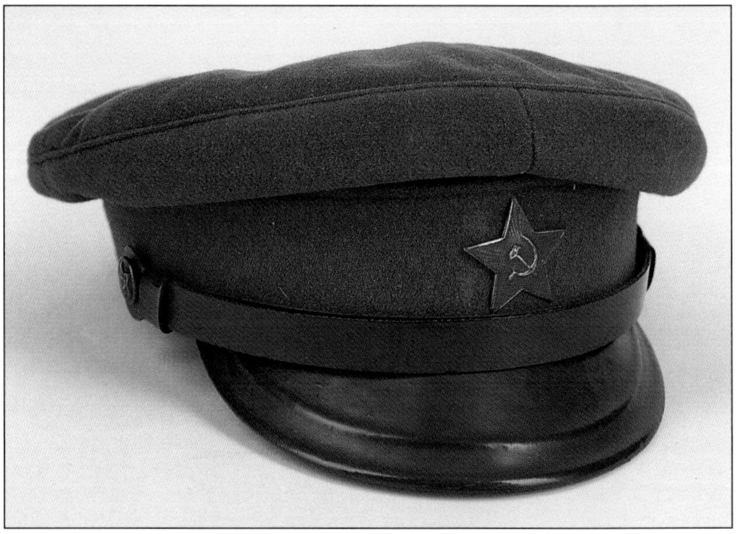

Variation of 1920s visor cap.

Air Force visor cap constructed like an Army cap using blue wool for Air Force. Acceptance stamp inside cap is dated 1927.

NKVD Border Troops visor cap. Left: Inside of NKVD visor cap shows a 1939 date. This example was probably reissued.

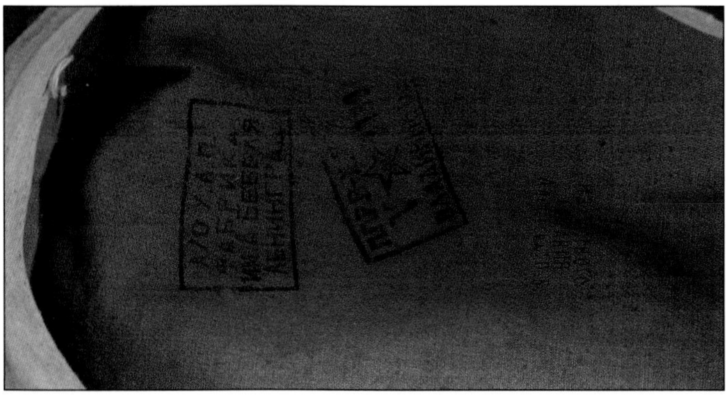

Cavalry cap with standard colors. During the 1920s many cavalry formations preserved their individuality by wearing colors specific to their group.

Leather helmet worn by an Armored Train Machine Gunner. Buttons are 1924 regulation black paint and the lining is blue cotton.

CHAPTER TWO

1935-1940

In 1935 new regulations decreed changes in insignia for Commanders and Senior Commanders. The introduction of sleeve chevrons was a significant improvement for recognition of personnel in leadership positions. Visor caps were now incorporating branch colors for all services. New patterns of leather belts and improved uniforms for service and field dress were introduced.

Just as major changes in the uniforms and insignia were being adopted to bring back the concept of a rank and file military organization, traditional titles were being reestablished in the officer ranks. The senior ranks were still considered to be "senior commanders" but the term general officer was still not used due to its aristocratic connotation. The status of "officer" was then restored for leadership of the "Peoples and Peasants Army" – officer classes then began using collar tabs and sleeve stripes to denote rank. Diamond shaped collar devices were used in combination with gold chevrons for Senior Commanders. Field grade officer ranks used rectangular enamel devices along with gold and red chevrons for colonel and red chevrons for other ranking officers. Junior officer ranks used red enamel squares for lieutenant in conjunction with red chevrons on the lower sleeve. The title of sergeant was returned to the senior enlisted grades of personnel at this time. The title "Marshal of the Soviet Union", the highest military rank, was conceived and bestowed.

Marshal of the Soviet Union service and field dress.

Marshal of the Soviet Union collar insignia introduced December 1935.

Marshal of the Soviet Union with sleeve insignia also introduced December 1935.

Marshal of the Soviet Union service dress, optional gray.

Collar, Marshal of the Soviet Union.

Sleeve insignia, Marshal of the Soviet Union.

Army Commander 1st Rank. This example is NKVD Frontier Troops.

Army Commander 1st Rank.

Sleeve insignia, Army Commander 1st Rank.

Army Commander 2nd Rank wore diamond shaped collar devices. These diamonds were used for the highest ranks of the Soviet system. During the period between 1935 and 1940, personnel that wore the diamond shaped devices were called Senior Commanders.

Army Commander 2nd Rank.

Army Commander 2nd Rank, note sleeve chevrons number the same as collar diamonds.

Army Commander 2nd Rank, Political Commissar.

Political Commissar collar tabs were the same color piping as the lower ranks. Gold edging was not used.

The Red Star with hammer and sickle was standard insignia for all commissars.

Mongolian Officers belt. There is photographic evidence of some Soviet Officers wearing these belts during campaigns against Japan in the 1930s.

Air Force Corps Commander. The tunic was commonly referred to as a "French." A British General named French was the original designer of this tunic style.

Collar tabs of Air Force Corps Commander.

Sleeve insignia of "Red Airmen."

Sleeve chevrons are sewn to a patch before application to the tunic.

Air Force Corps Commander. Greatcoat collar tabs had a different shape than collar tabs for a tunic. The branch of service color is indicated by the collar tabs and the cloth star on the budenovka. The holster shown is for a Nagant revolver.

Insignia for Air Force is wings and a single propeller.

Sleeve insignia of the Red Airmen was worn on the left sleeve of the greatcoat. Sleeve chevrons on this greatcoat are the same size as chevrons on the tunic. However, chevrons worn on greatcoats were sometimes larger.

Air Force Corps Commander field uniform.

Collar of Air Force Corps Commander.

Pilot insignia.

Division Commissar Armor Forces.

Tank Division Commissar.

Insignia of Commissar.

Division Commander, Armor Forces.

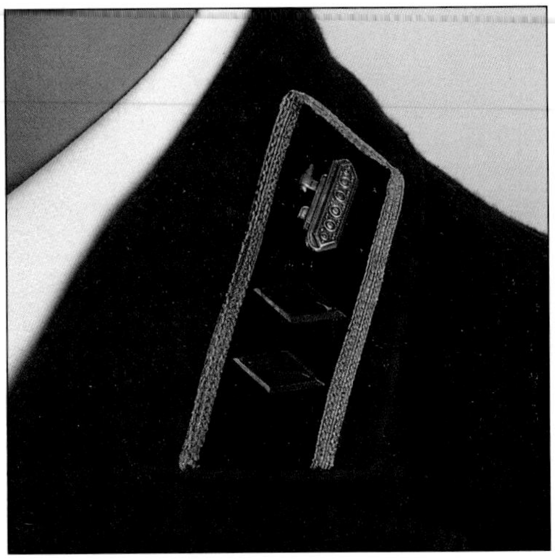

Tank Division Commander.

Sleeve Chevrons for Division Commander.

Air Force Division Commander.

Air Division Commander.

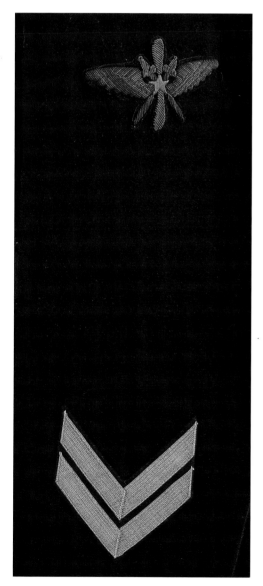

Sleeve of Division Commander with Flight Status.

Army Commander, Division Commander. This style introduced in 1936 was worn by command and educational personnel of the W&PRA General Staff Academy.

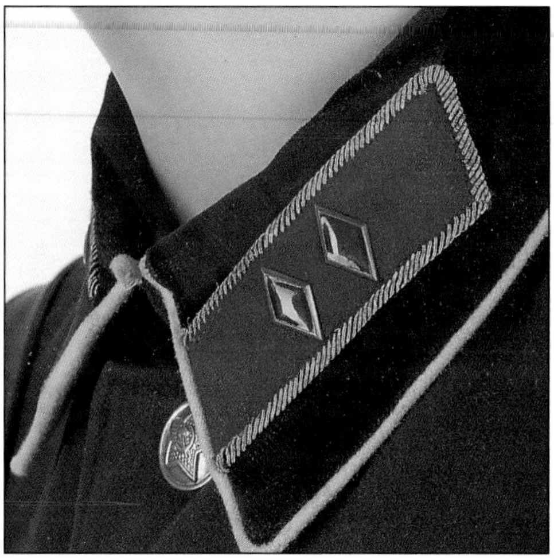

A black collar with white piping are the branch colors of the General Staff Academy.

In this example the sleeve chevrons are sewn directly to the tunic.

Army Brigade Commander of Infantry Field Service.

A single diamond on collar tabs denotes Brigade Commander.

Sleeve Chevron of Brigade Commander.

Model 1935 Brigade Commissar of NKVD Frontier troops.

Senior Commissar colors of NKVD Frontier troops. *(Photos this page by Les Kirby)*

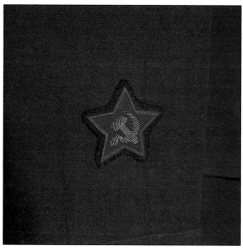

Commissar sleeve insignia.

NKVD Senior Official Service Dress.

Brick red is branch color for State Security.

Sleeve insignia of NKVD State Security Official.

NKVD Senior Official of Administration.

Senior Official of NKVD.

Sleeve insignia of NKVD Senior Official.

Naval Admiral of Engineering, parade dress, 1940.

Collar of 1935 Admiral. *(Photos this page by Les Kirby)*

Sleeve of Rear Admiral.

Naval Captain service dress, 1935-1943. Line officers used gold insignia and technical personnel wore silver insignia.

Note the sleeve rings going from seam to seam on the sleeve. These rings were replaced with a sleeve patch in 1943.

Major Air Force service dress.

The two rectangles on collar tab denote Major. The branch color and corps emblem are for Air Force.

Two crossed swords are the insignia of pilot.

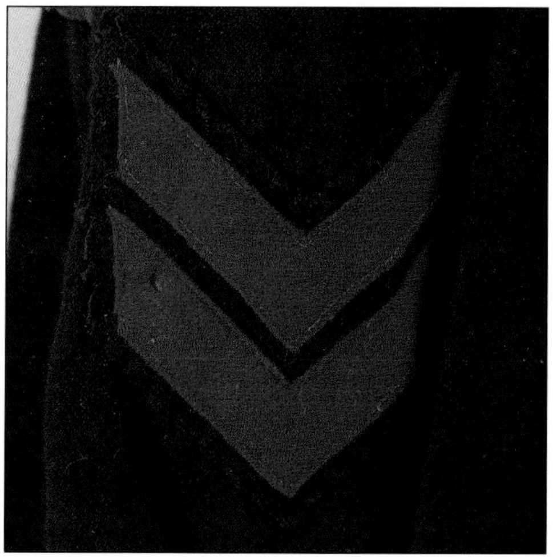

The rank of Major wore two wide red chevrons on the sleeve. Junior officers wore a narrower chevron.

Army Political Commissar, rank of Lieutenant Colonel.

Three rectangles denote Lieutenant Colonel.

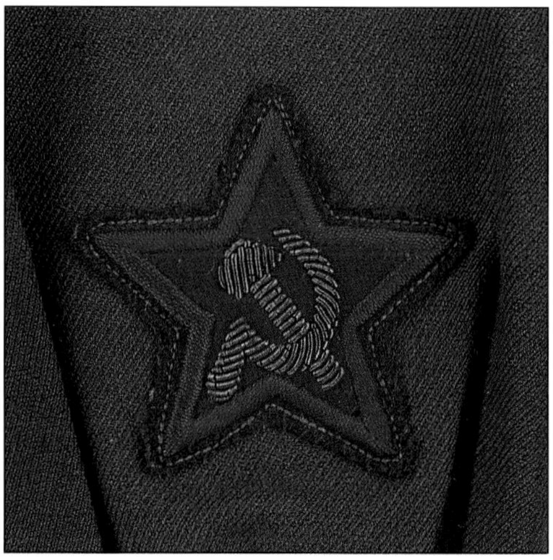

Commissar Sleeve stars were worn on both sleeves.

This coat has a detachable back strap.

Army Greatcoat for Lieutenant Colonel.

Left above: Collar tab shape on great coats is common for all ranks until 1943.
Left: Political Commissar star.

Full length leather coat for flight personnel.

The two rectangles on the collar tab denote the rank of Major.

Sleeve insignia of Air Engineer. A hammer and wrench are used on engineer insignia.

Medical Corps Major tunic and Budionovka. Note green star on cap. The lower patch pockets shown here were being phased out in 1935.

The collar tabs are dark green with red edging and carry the Medical insignia.

The sleeve has a two button cuff. Note the lower patch pocket.

This pattern of uniform for political personnel was unchanged through 1942.

Colored piping on collar tabs was a feature worn by political personnel. Metallic gold trim was not worn by the political personnel.

The Red Star emblem worn on both sleeves denoted political officer.

Captain of Infantry Rifles.

Target and crossed rifles insignia was earned for superior tactical maneuvers.

Sleeve insignia for Captain.

Right: Senior Sergeants with Field Kit. The dark gymnastiorka is wool and the light one is cotton.

Armor Colonel wearing steel gray tunic. Note unusual position of "XX" Anniversary Medal.

Naval Enlisted man summer dress. Note anchors at end of ribbon. Photo dated 1938.

Right: Air Force Officers. Captain is wearing Sport Paratrooper badge.

Senior Political Advisor summer service.

Artillery collar tabs. Branch of Service emblem was worn but wasn't regulation for political personnel.

Political Officer sleeve stars. In 1942, Germany issued the "Commissar Order", a death sentence for anyone captured wearing these stars on their uniform.

Naval Enlisted Mans Jumper, summer dress.

Back view of Naval Summer Jumper.

Label and Internal Stamp of Naval jumper.

Militia Pattern Gymnastiorka.

Collar tabs worn by Militia member. The Militia served as police and maintained portions of the Gulag prison system.

NKVD Senior NCO. Black buttons on the tunic were replaced with brass in the late 1930s.

The four triangles on the collar tabs denote the highest non-commissioned rank.

Sergeant Sniper service dress. Only snipers wore the distinctive colored vertical panel on the front of the Gymnastiorka.

Raspberry collar tabs and black piping were worn by enlisted personnel of the Infantry. The single triangle denotes sergeant.

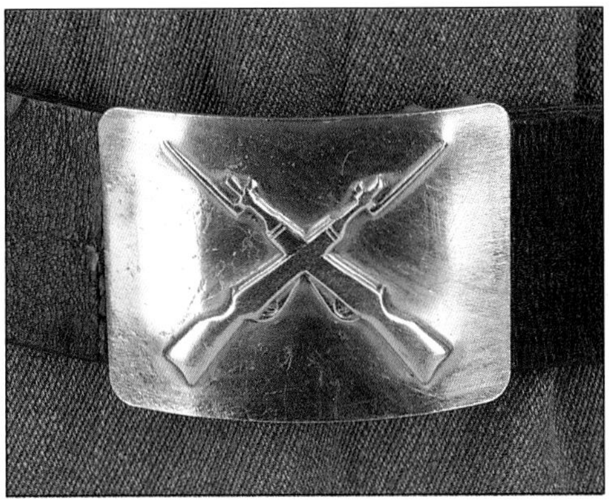

A non-standard belt with "Rifles" insignia.

Armored Junior Lieutenant Field Uniform. This leather jacket is a variation similar to many worn during this period. The red border on the collar tabs is most often used with NCOs. Promotion was often done in the field with rank devices only.

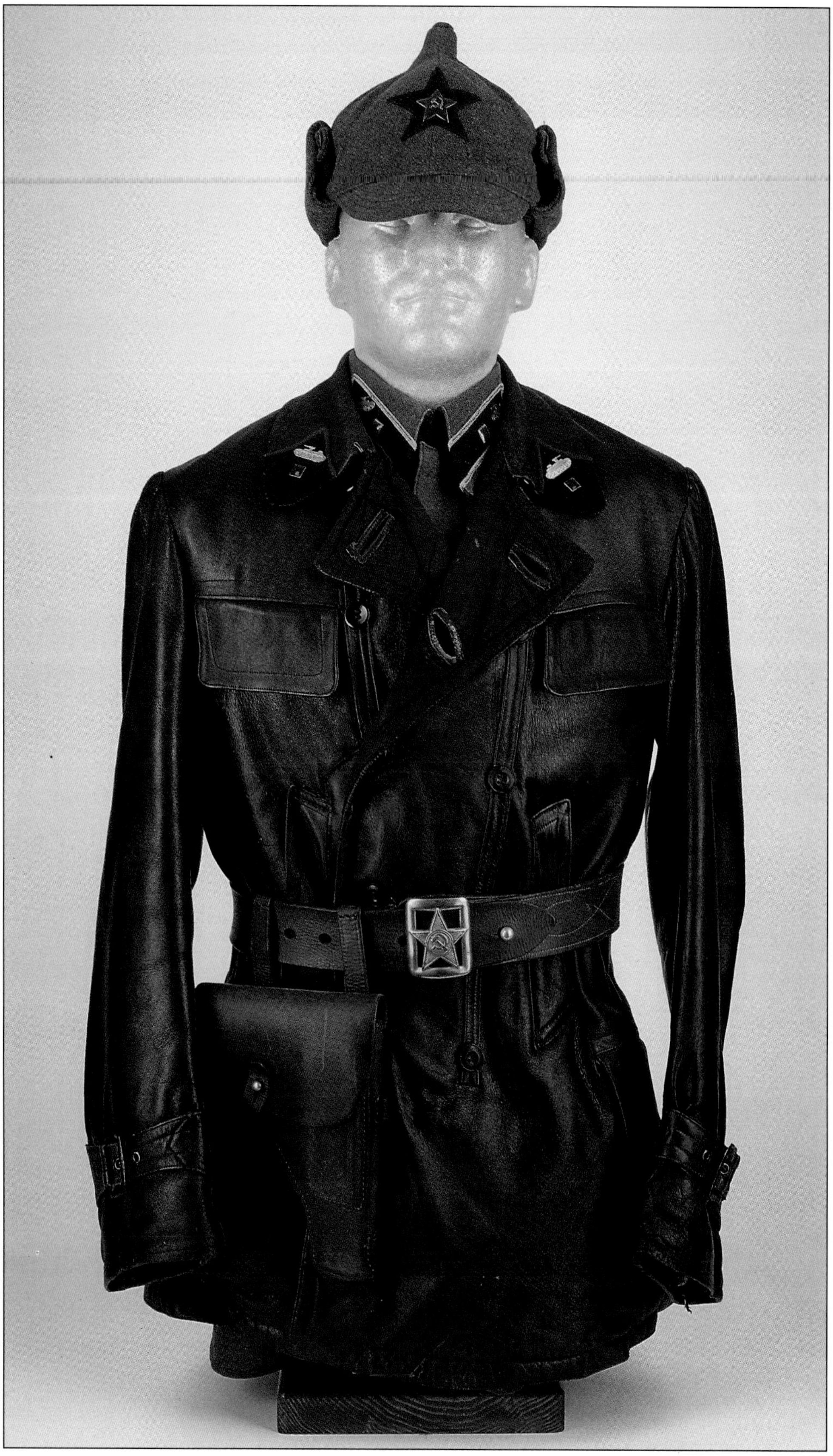

Militia Captain introduced in 1938. The militia operated similar to a police force.

Collar tabs have a single rectangle of blue enamel.

The sleeve insignia is the "Eleven Republics" pattern. There is one ribbon at the base of the symbol of the Soviet Union and five on each side of the blue enamel field. This pattern was used from 1937 to 1947.

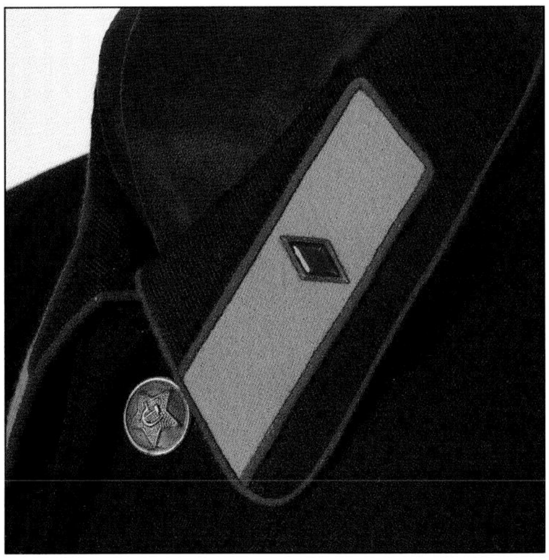

Collar tab of Senior Official of the Militia.

NKVD Intelligence Department of State Security.

NKVD Rank equivalent to Lieutenant.

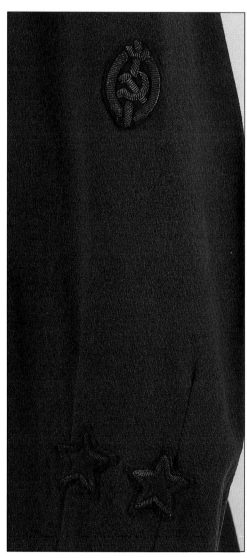

Right: Upper and lower Sleeve insignia of an NKVD Official. The lower sleeve stars correspond to the collar tab stars. These sleeve stars, denoting rank, could be seen at a greater distance than the tabs. Use of the sleeve stars was discontinued before 1940.

Tunic of the NKVD Air Force.

Collar tabs are rank of Junior Lieutenant.

Upper Sleeve insignia of NKVD Pilot.

Single star of Junior Lieutenant. Lower sleeve insignia are command insignia.

NKVD State Security colors were brick red and raspberry. Piping around the collar and cuffs was only for commanders and Senior Commanders of all branches of the NKVD. Visor cap has light blue top.

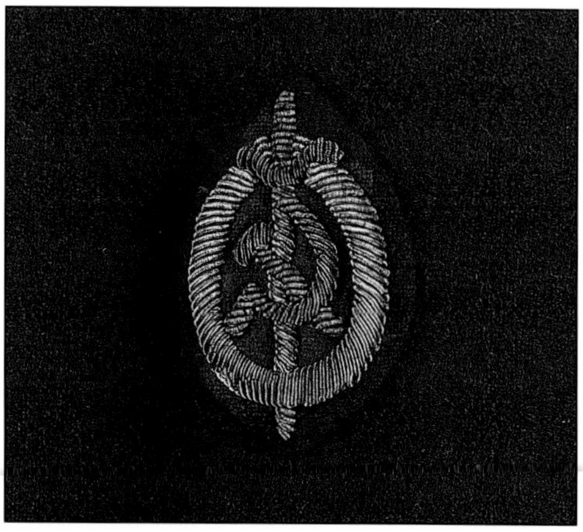

Insignia of State Security official.

NKVD Official sleeve insignia variation with main office indicated by the larger size.

Collar tabs with brick red and raspberry were the most common colors for NKVD.

Wool blend salt and pepper fabric for NKVD.

Right: NKVD Officer.

Below: Leadership group of NKVD circa 1938.

NKVD dress for female personnel.

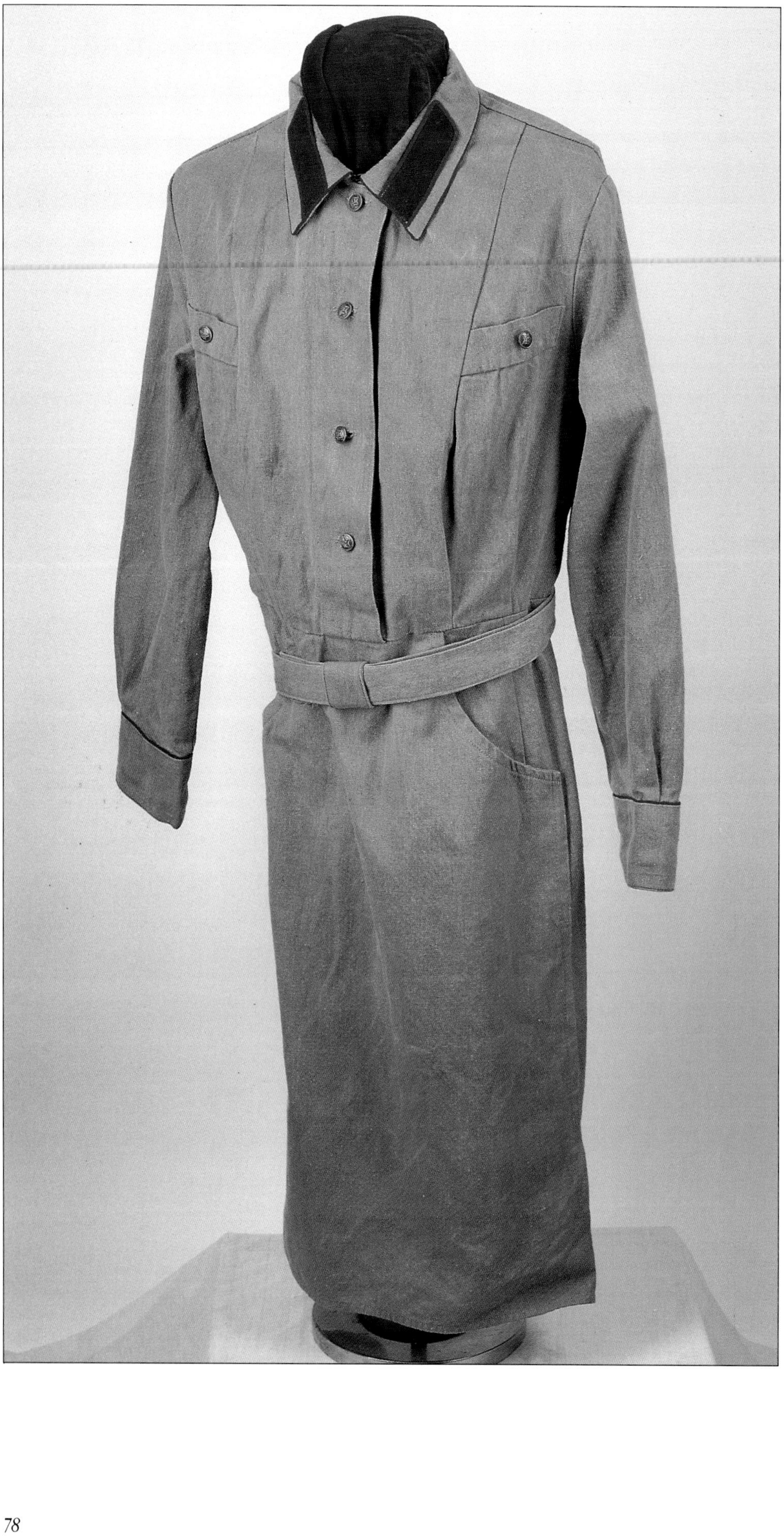

Collar of Woman's Tunic.

NKVD Mid Grade Official.

The woven fabric shown here is "salt and pepper." In the 1930s, various shades of this fabric were used by organizations including the Military.

Insignia of NKVD.

Air Force Lieutenant field dress. The pilotka (cap) was dark blue for Air Force.

Two squares on collar tabs indicate Lieutenant.

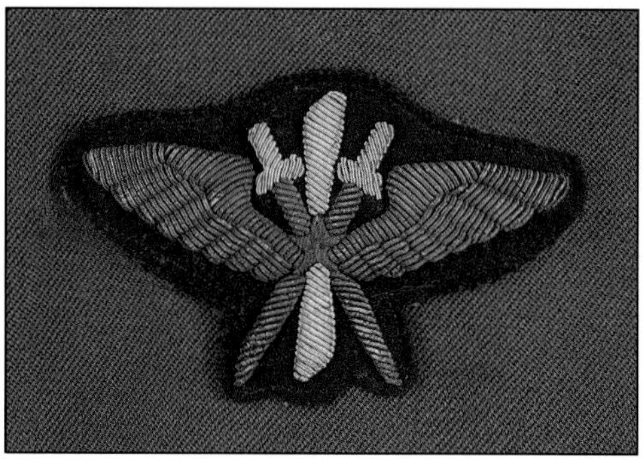

Insignia worn on upper sleeve by pilots.

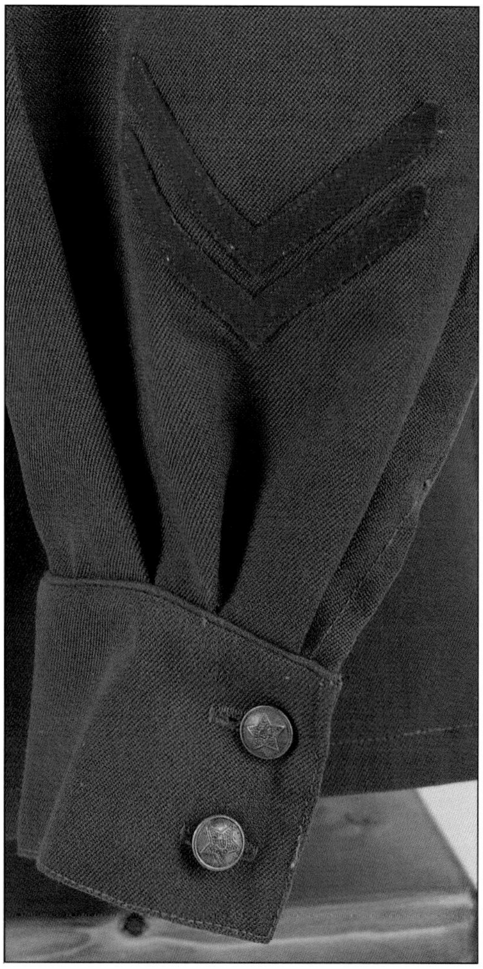

Right: Two red chevrons on lower sleeve indicate Lieutenant.

Junior Politruk of Infantry.

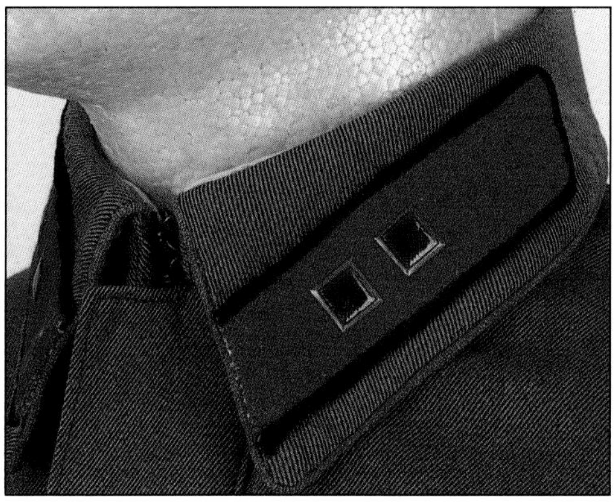

Political personnel did not use gold metallic edging on collar tabs.

Insignia of Political Personnel worn on the lower sleeve.

Right: Air Force Specialty Officer at right. Note Political Officer insignia without rank devices. Specialty personnel were often Photography, Correspondence, etc.

Above: A group of four sergeants circa 1939. The belts they are wearing were usually reserved for commanders.

Right: Air Force enlisted men. Note exposed buttons on left and hidden buttons on right. The hidden buttons are of earlier regulation. Photo dated 1935.

Right: Soldiers in service dress, 1938.

Sergeant of Armor Forces, 1940.

A center stripe was added to collar tabs in 1940. In November of that year a triangle was added to distinguish the NCO insignia.

Army private of Signals.

Collar of Signals private.

CHAPTER THREE

1940-1943

In 1940 the status of General was restored to senior military personnel. The diamond shaped insignia of Senior Commander was replaced with the five pointed star for the new status of General. Officer ranks adopted a new sleeve chevron with combinations of red and gold for all officer ranks. A new pattern of steel helmet and additional field equipment was introduced to give the Soviets the look of a more modern military.

Marshal of the Soviet Union service dress Model 1940.

The wreath, hammer and sickle were added in to the collar tab design in 1940.

Red backing was added to sleeve stars and sleeve chevrons were enhanced.

Marshal of Soviet Union, service dress Gymnastiorka.

Marshal of the Soviet Union.

Sleeve insignia of Marshal of the Soviet Union.

A new pattern of button using the Seal of the Soviet Union with the eleven Republics was introduced for Marshal and General uniforms. This example is the small button type.

General of the Army. In 1940 lower outside pockets were eliminated and the upper pocket were tailored internally with no pocket flaps.

A new pattern of button using the Seal of the Soviet Union showing eleven Republics became regulation for all Generals and Marshals tunics. The example shown is the large button type.

Sleeve Insignia of General of the Army.

General of the Army. This tunic was made in an optional gray color. Many Generals wore gray as walking out dress.

Collar of General of the Army.

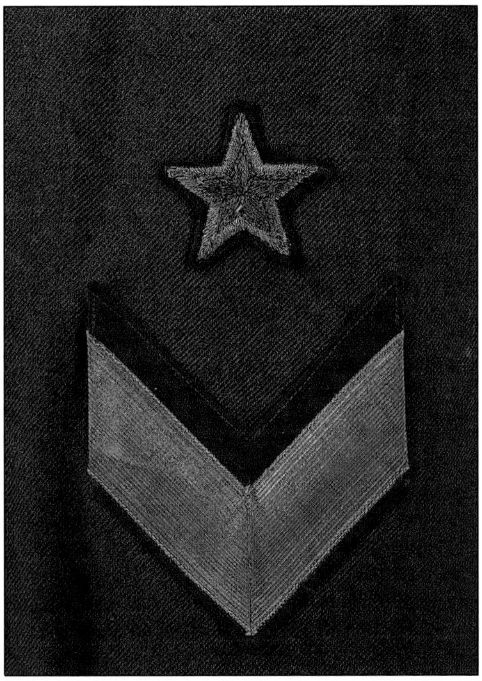

Sleeve of General of the Army.

Army Lieutenant General parade dress 1940. This was a new uniform intended to give improved recognition to General Officer ranks. The belt used with this specific uniform did not have the holes and stud for adjustment.

Collar tabs of Lieutenant General of the Artillery.

Sleeve insignia of Model 1940 General parade tunic.

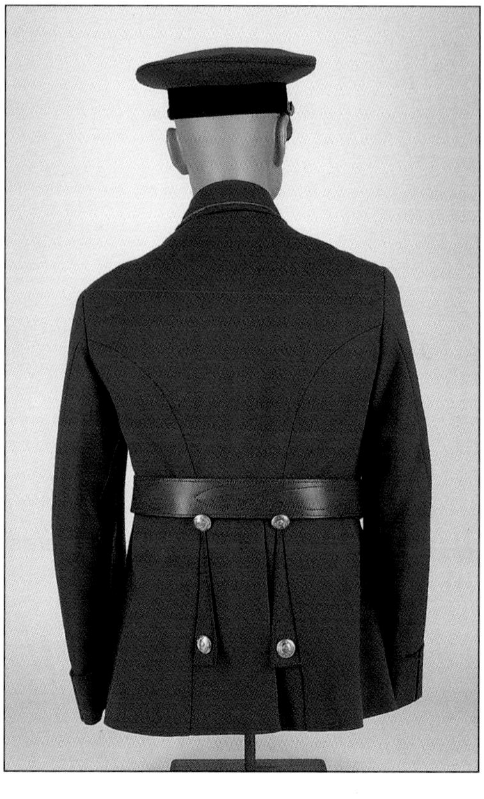

Right: Back view of the Model 1940 General Officers uniform.

Army Lieutenant General summer dress 1940.

Collar tab for Army Lieutenant General with three stars. Major General wore two stars on the collar tab and Colonel General wore four stars.

This pattern of sleeve insignia was worn by Generals up to the rank of General of the Army (Five Stars).

Lieutenant General field service 1941. Subdued insignia was introduced in 1941 throughout the Army. Distribution of this insignia was not extensive and the more colorful insignia were used until 1943.

Branch color was not used on the collar tabs. Branch insignia devices were worn when appropriate.

The new subdued button with the eleven Republics.

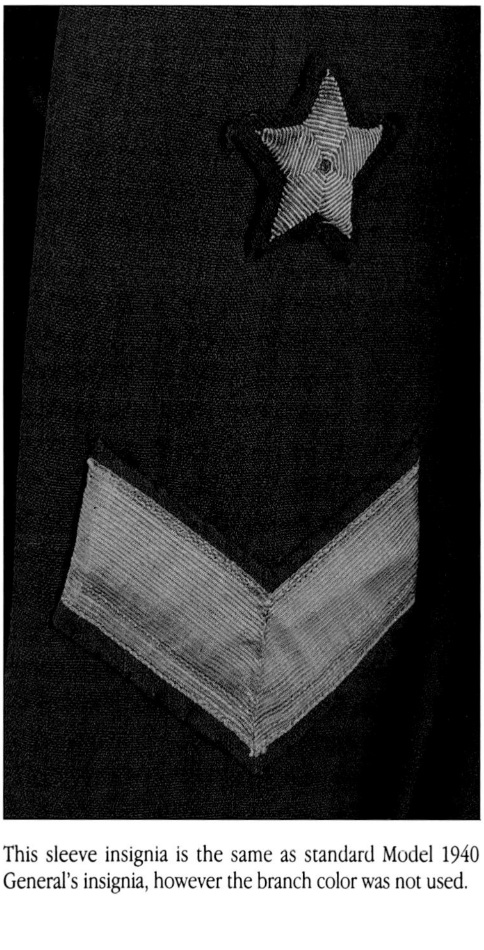

This sleeve insignia is the same as standard Model 1940 General's insignia, however the branch color was not used.

Air Force Lieutenant General service dress Model 1940.

Collar of Air Force Lieutenant General.

Sleeve insignia of Model 1940 Air Force General.

Army Major General service and field dress 1940.

Infantry Generals did not use corps emblem on collar tabs.

Rank insignia was always worn on both sleeves.

Army Major General 1940. The darker color is the only difference between this tunic and the previous Army Major General tunic.

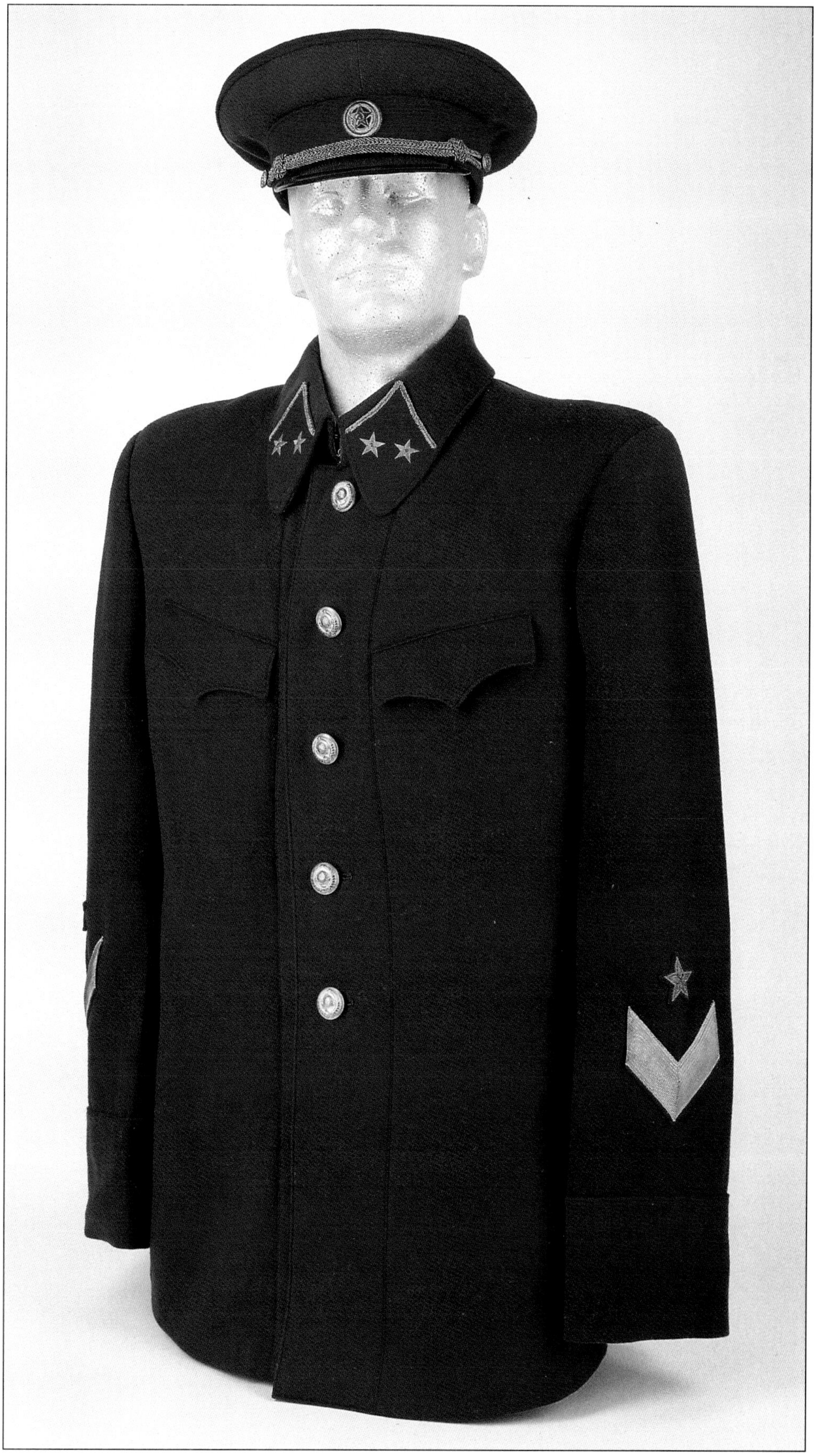

Collar of Major General of Infantry with a construction variation.

Sleeve of Model 1940 General.

Artillery Major General Model 1940.

Black velvet collar tabs with gilt stars. *(Photos this page by Les Kirby)*

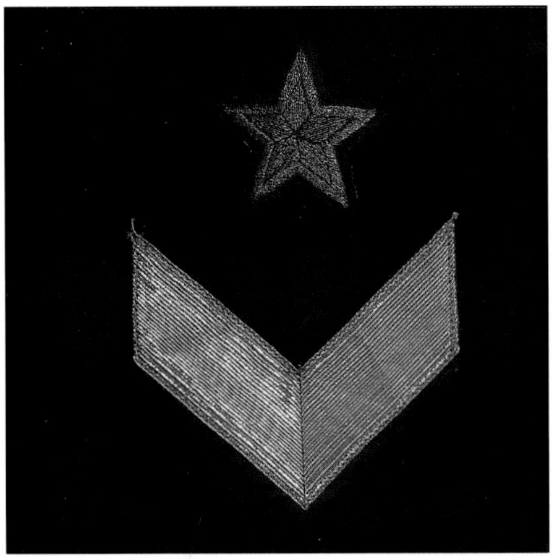

Sleeve insignia of Artillery General, 1940.

Major General Military Intelligence. These troops performed functions similar to the Military Police.

Dark blue is the branch color of the Military Intelligence.

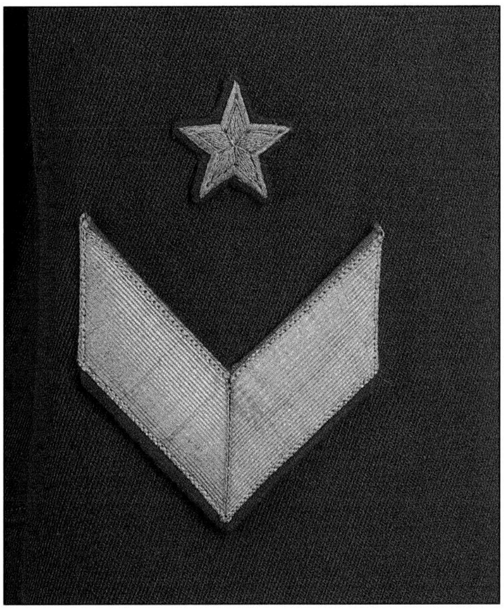

The dark blue backing on the sleeve insignia was extended to NKVD Troops.

Army Major General service dress uniform with gymnastiorka.

Collar of infantry General gymnastiorka.

Sleeve insignia of General Officers gymnastiorka.

Air Force service dress for Major General.

Collar of Air Force Major General.

Sleeve insignia of Model 1940 Air Force General.

Army Major General of Artillery.

Army Major General of Armor wearing the gray uniform for service and field dress.

Collar of Armor General.

Navy Rear Admiral of Aviation.

Upper sleeve insignia of the Red Airman on a naval uniform.

Admirals wore a star with hammer and sickle on the lower sleeve. The branch color is between the sleeve rings.

Infantry Colonel service and field dress 1940.

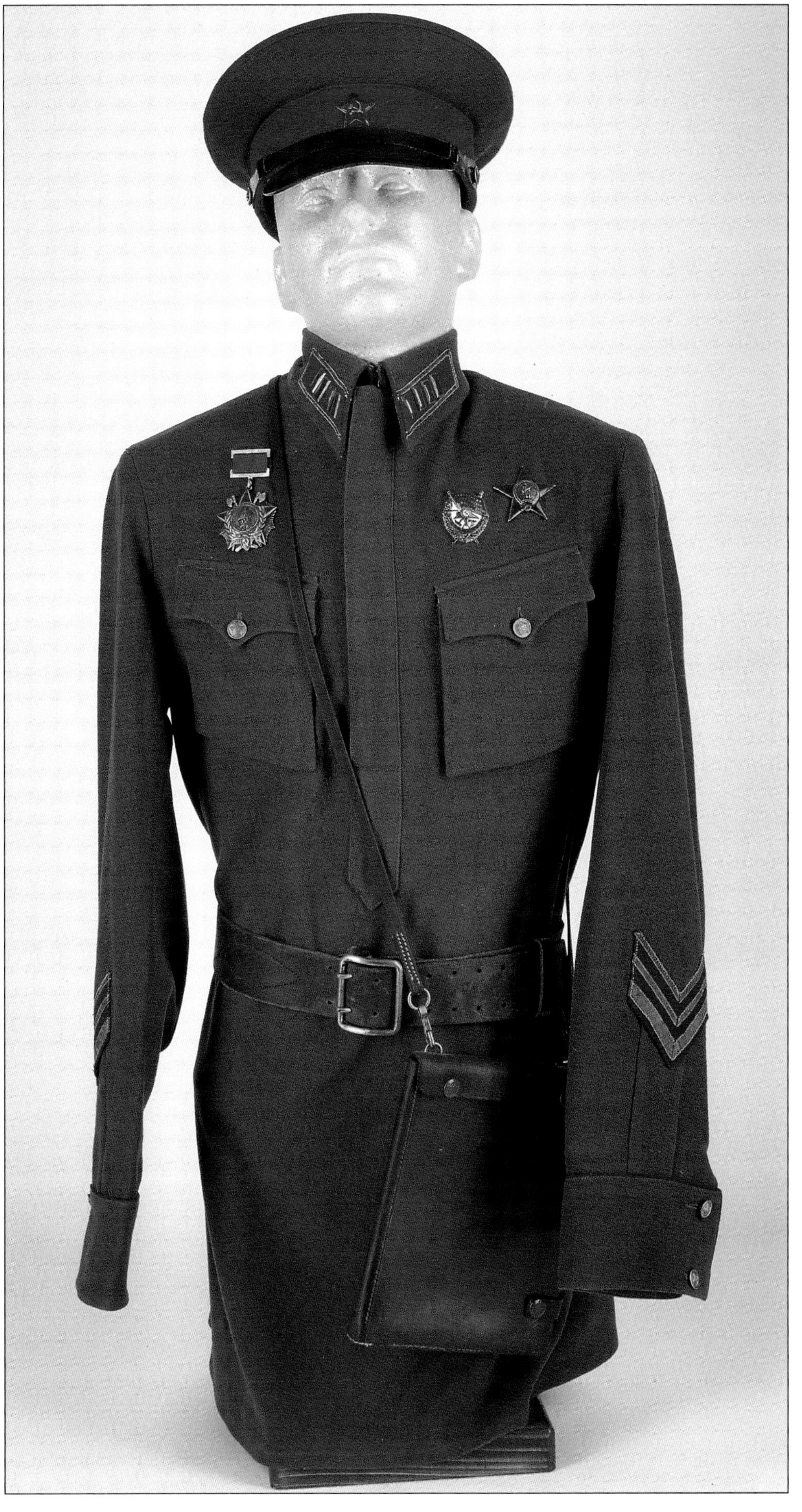

The four enamel rectangles on collar tabs denote rank of Full Colonel.

Sleeve chevron worn by Full Colonel.

Right: Senior Colonel of Artillery, 1940.

Admiral parade dress circa 1941.

Right: The Lieutenant Colonel on the left is wearing a Tokarev bayonet on his belt along with a handgun. Summer 1942.

Army Major Infantry Rifles service,1940 with pleated pockets.

Two enamel rectangles indicate Major. The rifles insignia is a badge of proficiency recognition for the regiment.

Sleeve chevron for the rank of Major.

Cavalry Major, 1940. Dark blue and black were the colors for cavalry of the regular army. The corps insignia is a horse head and crossed swords. The leather rig shown here is a field belt kit introduced in 1932.

Rank devices were prong back or screw back.

Below: Holster for TT33 Tokarev Semi-automatic pistol.

Sleeve chevrons for Major.

Below: The larger styles of map cases were worn either this way or with a shoulder strap.

A strap sewn inside the top strap is holding the shoulder strap assembly.

Artillery Major 1940. Black and red are the branch colors for artillery.

Black collar tabs with crossed cannon denote Artillery.

Major rank sleeve chevron.

Army Major Infantry Rifles. Model 1935 tunic with sleeve chevrons updated to 1940 regulation.

Two enamel rectangles indicate the rank of Major.

1940 sleeve chevron denoting rank of Major.

Air Force Major Service Dress 1940. This pattern of tunic was introduced in 1935. Embroidered insignia on the visor cap was introduced in 1938 for Air Force Officers. The dark blue "French" tunic and the Gymnastiorka were phased out in 1942.

Light blue collar tabs with winged propeller are branch color and insignia for Air Forces.

Upper sleeve insignia of the Red Airman.

Sleeve chevrons, rank of Major updated to 1940 regulations.

Army Major Infantry Rifles. Crossed rifles and target indicated "Rifle" Status, a badge of honor for the regiment that was replaced in 1942 by the army with the Guards Badge. The lower pockets were eliminated from the 1935 design and internal pockets and button down flaps replaced the upper patch pockets.

Infantry Rifles collar tabs for rank of Major.

Sleeve chevron for rank of Major.

NKVD blocking troops, 1940.

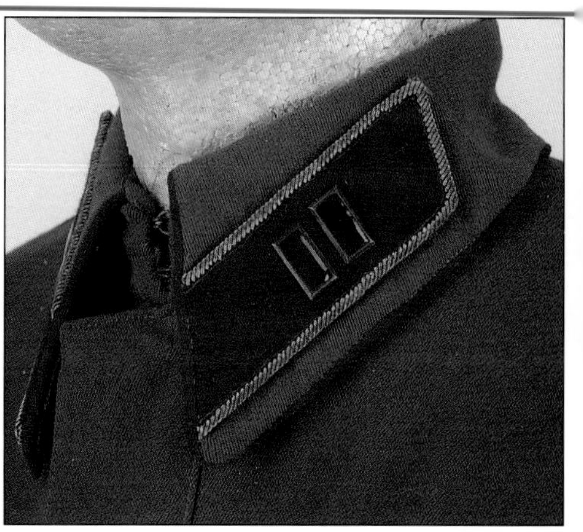

Collar tabs using brick red branch color for NKVD.

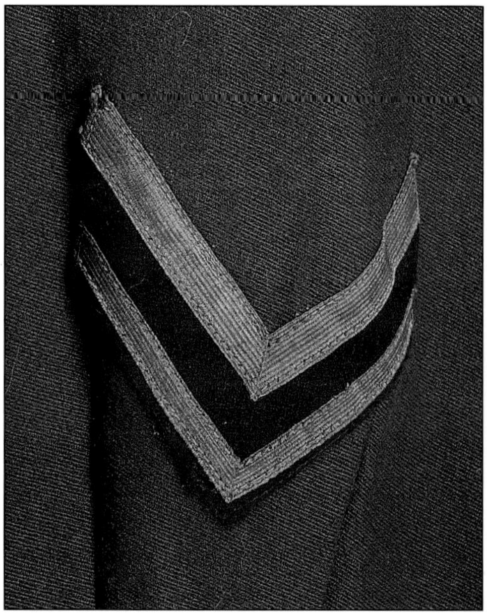

These sleeve chevrons are an example of a short lived design used by the NKVD. Two colors are used on this insignia.

Air Force Captain service dress. This gymnastiorka is made from a type of fabric popular before the war.

Collar of Air Force Captain.

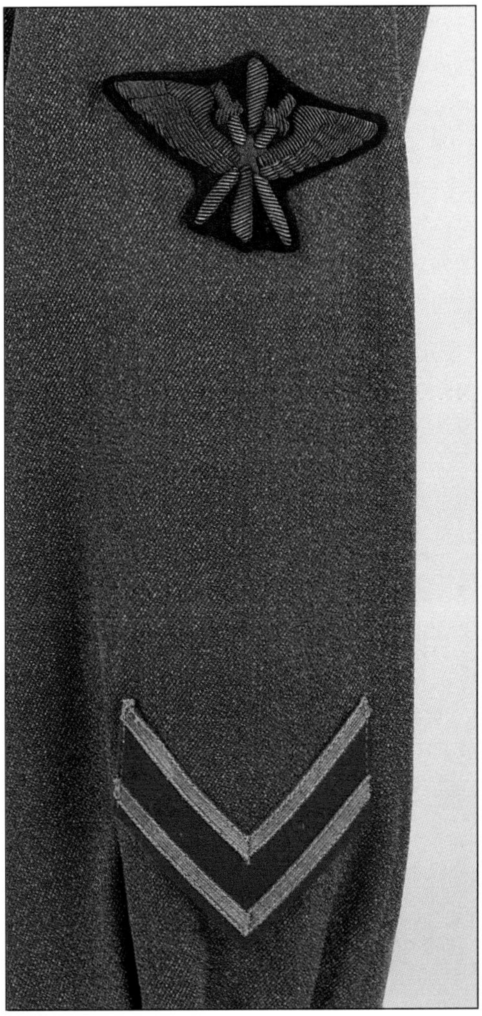

Left: Sleeve of Air Force Flying Officer.

Air Force Captain 1940 uniform worn as field and service dress becoming more common as service dress during the phase out of the dark blue uniform.

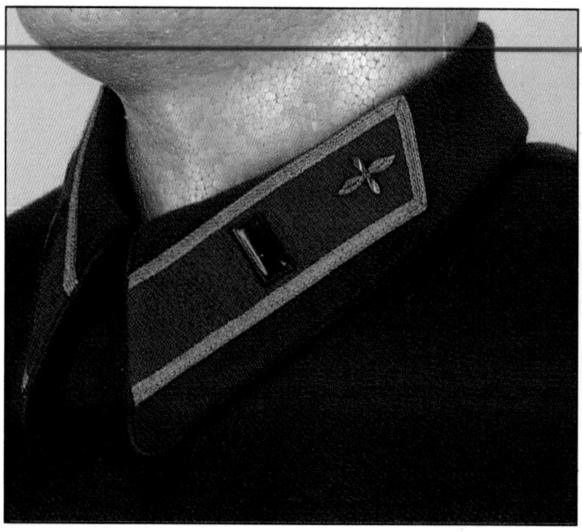

Collar tabs are light blue with Air Force corps insignia and enamel rectangle for rank of Captain.

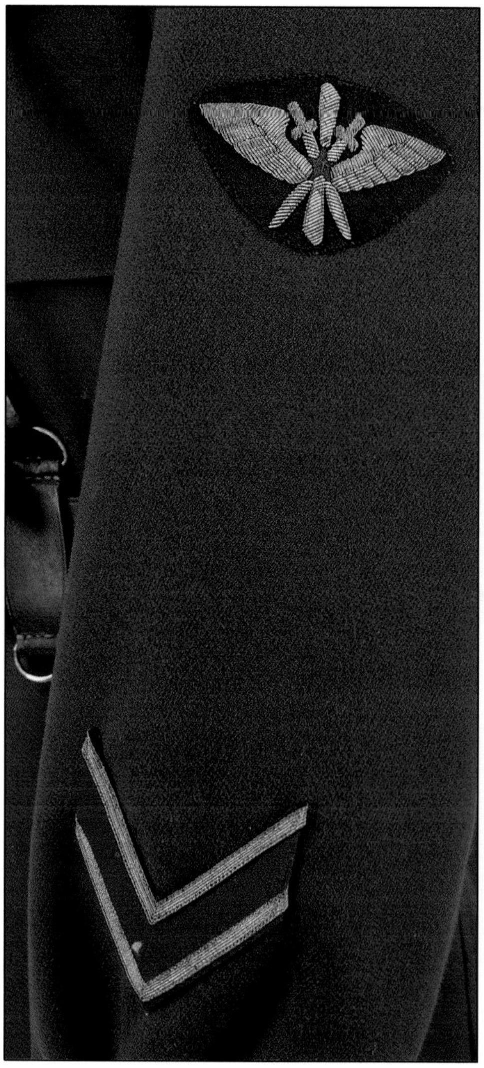

Right: Sleeve insignia of Red Airman with sleeve chevron rank of Captain.

Right: Officers in the field, 1942.

Engineer Officers, 1942.

Below: Artillery Officers, 1942.

Army Medical Captain. This example does not have sleeve chevrons as per 1941 regulations.

Collar tabs are in dark green and red, branch colors for Medical and Administration personnel. Addition of corps emblem indicates specific branch.

Infantry Captain summer service with no sleeve chevrons per 1941 regulations.

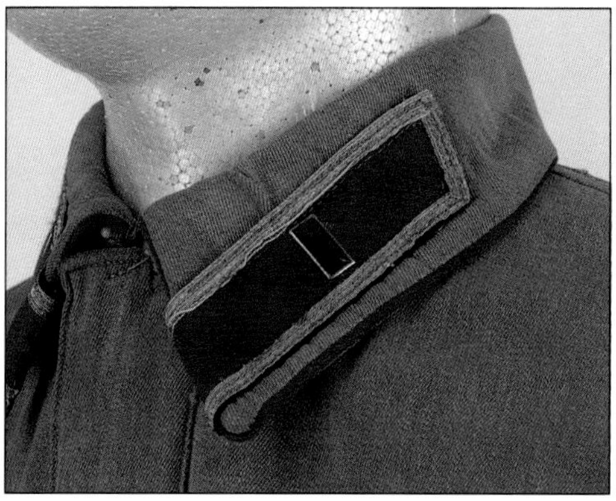

Captain Command Personnel collar tabs. Tape was used instead of twisted wire for piping.

Transportation Captain Gymnastiorka 1940. No sleeve chevrons were applied per August 1941 regulations.

Black velvet collar tabs with light blue piping and single rectangle for rank of Captain with Transportation corps insignia.

Army Engineer Captain service uniform.

Some Technical personnel did not wear the gold trimmed collar tabs of command status.

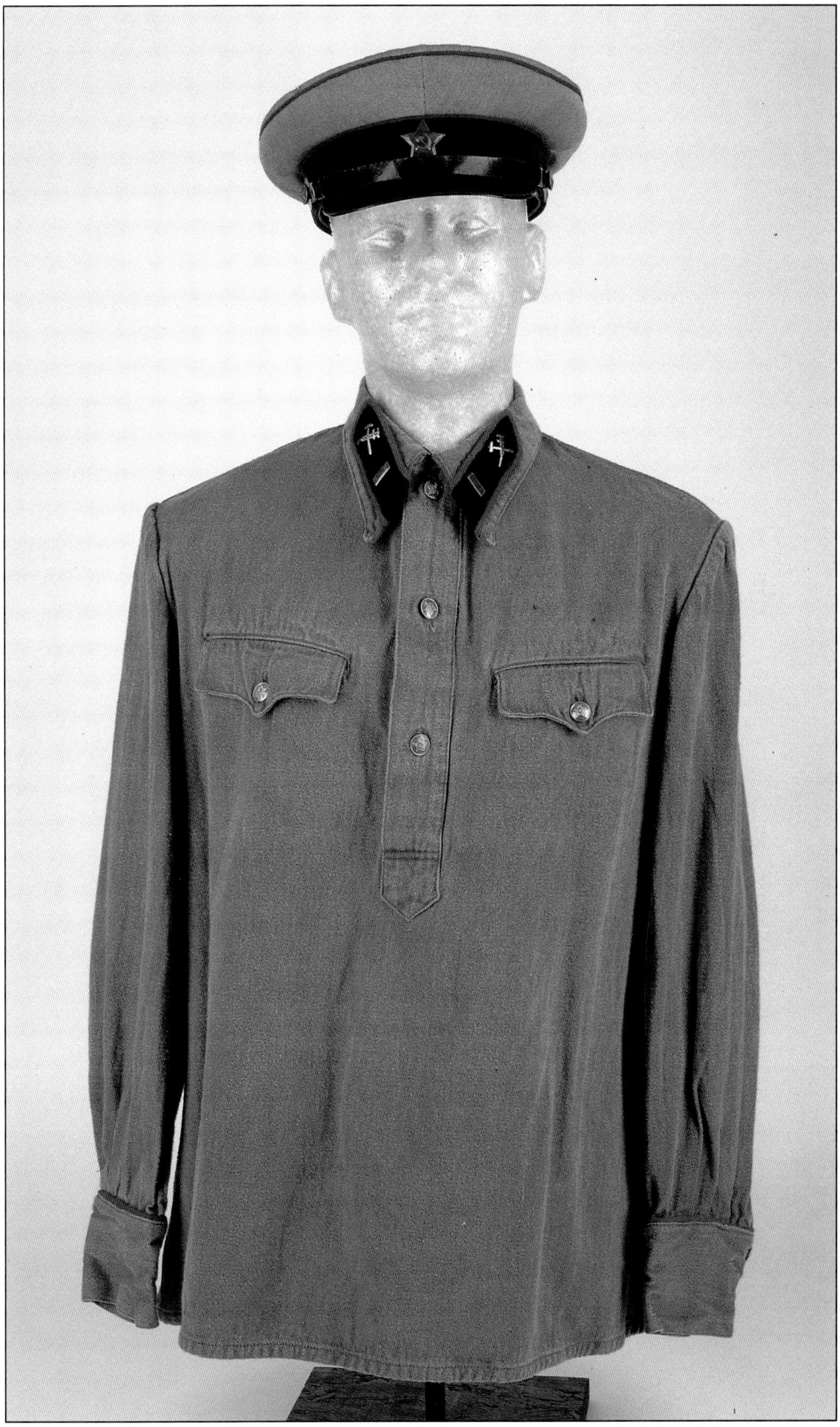

Armor Captain 1940. Steel gray was adopted for Armor personnel in recognition of their elite status.

The single enamel rectangle on black velvet with Armored Troops insignia was worn by Captain Armored troops.

Sleeve chevron for rank of Captain.

Armor Captain Leathers 1935-1943. Due to shortages of material during the early war years, these patterns were replaced with similar articals of canvas.

This pattern collar tab was commonly worn on greatcoats from 1935 through 1942.

A field made Officers service belt. It was hand hammered and cut out. The chasing on the star is also done by hand. The hammer and sickle device is riveted to the star. It is believed that this belt was produced in Leningrad during the siege.

Captain NKVD Frontier Troops. The leather kit is the 1932 pattern. The visor cap dates from the 1920s. Since there were basically no color changes, these older caps were used until supplies of the new caps were available.

Emerald green collar tabs and cap crown were distinguishing features of the Frontier Troops.

Sleeve Chevron for rank of Captain.

Winter service for Lieutenant of Infantry, 1941.

Army Officers in winter 1941-1942.

Note Political sleeve stars and rank chevrons. Some are without sleeve insignia and a variety of belts are worn.

Senior Lieutenant Sappers summer field service. During 1941-1942 Gymnastiorkas were being issued without piping on the collar and cuffs. This is particularly noticeable with junior officers.

Three enamel squares on collar tabs show rank of senior lieutenant and corps insignia show Sappers branch.

Sleeve chevrons were used on this tunic contrary to regulations for this time period. These denote rank of Senior Lieutenant.

Senior Lieutenant Air Force service dress 1940.

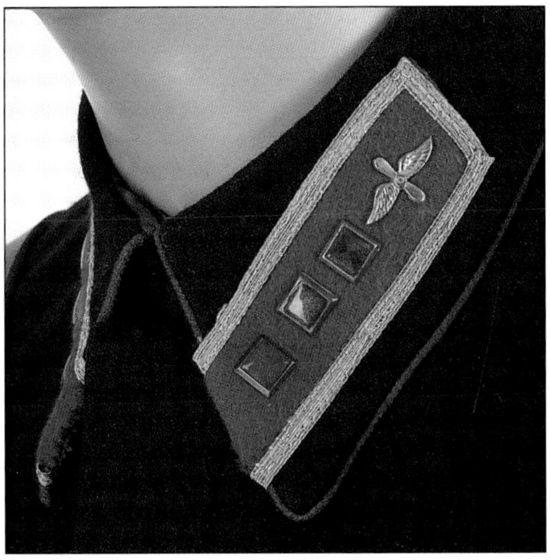

Three enamel squares to denote rank of Senior Lieutenant and corps insignia of Air Force on blue collar tab.

Upper sleeve insignia of Red Airman. The swords indicate Pilot.

Sleeve chevron for Senior Lieutenant Air Force.

Army Senior Lieutenant of Artillery.

Three enamel squares for rank insignia and crossed cannon for corps insignia. The twisted gilt wire that indicates Command Status.

Upper sleeve insignia of tank destruction personnel.

Sleeve insignia detail, Senior Lieutenant.

Lieutenant Armor service dress. This pattern "French" in steel gray was adopted in 1935.

Black velvet collar tabs with rank insignia and corps emblem. The most common way of wearing tank devices was with the tank pointing inward as shown here.

These sleeve chevrons were updated to 1940 regulations.

Lieutenant of Armor service dress with gymnastiorka.

Positioning of the tanks in this fashion was a popular practice.

Sleeve chevron of Lieutenant.

Army Infantry Lieutenant. This example is constructed of extra heavy fabric for wear in cold climates without a greatcoat.

Two enamel squares for Infantry Lieutenant.

Sleeve chevron for Lieutenant.

Army Engineers field service 1941 pattern. The subdued insignia was intended to replace the pre-war regulations. Though great numbers were issued, the pre-war insignia was worn until 1943.

Lieutenant Engineers collar tabs with rank insignia and corps identification.

Army Junior Lieutenant service and field dress 1940.

Infantry Junior Lieutenant single enamel square on collar tab.

Sleeve chevron for Army Junior Lieutenant.

Army Artillery Junior Lieutenant. This tunic is a Model 1935 with 1940 pattern sleeve chevrons.

Artillery Junior Lieutenant collar.

Sleeve Chevron of Junior Lieutenant.

The standing officer wears the regulation 1940 pattern service dress uniform.

Above: Berets were often worn by women soldiers. Photo dated 1942. Below: Troops in the field circa 1942.

NKVD NCO, 1940.

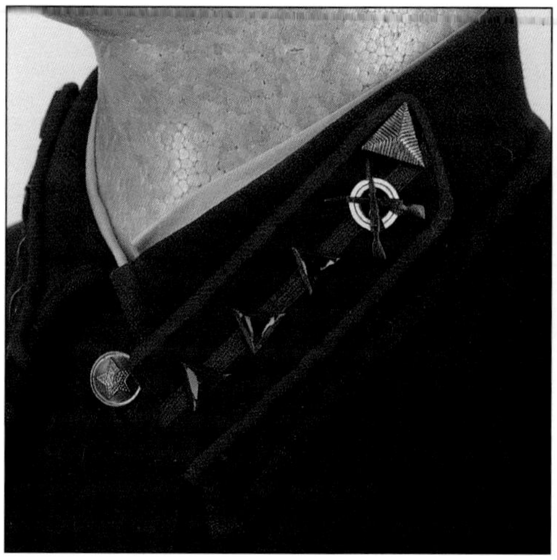

The gold triangle was added to the design of collar tabs for Sergeant.

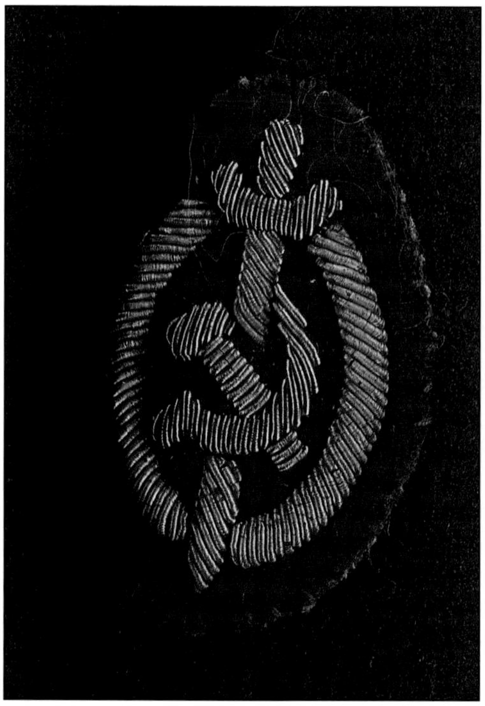

Insignia of State Security.

The subdued collar tab as worn by Air Force.

Air Force Sergeant 1st Class Engineering Technical Personnel with branch insignia introduced in April 1942. This women's tunic has the front panel buttons on the opposite side. A blue skirt was regulation and standard headgear was a beret with a Red Star but often women wore the "pilotka" cap.

Army Sergeant of Artillery field service. The ammunition pouches are an example of the many types used with 7.62 bolt action rifles. Note the Model 1940 helmet.

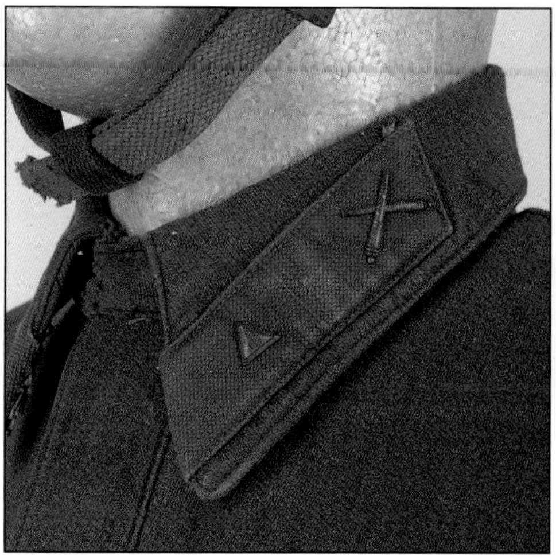

Rank insignia on the collar tabs are olive enamel instead of painted brass.

Right: Artillery Sergeant profile showing Model 1940 Helmet.

Cadet of Leningrad Artillery College uniform introduced in 1940.

The letters on the collar tab indicate school attended. This cadet wears the insignia of Sergeant.

Left: A brass triangle on collar tabs for NCOs was introduced in November 1940. Usage was not universal. Center: Infantry Rifles senior Sergeant, 1942. Right: Naval enlisted man service dress 1941.

Right: Cadet Recruits. Note that they don't have school or corps insignia, Summer 1940.

Right: In the field 1942.

Private field service with camouflage smock frequently used by snipers. This 1936 pattern helmet was used well into the war. The pouch is for Tokarev rifle magazines.

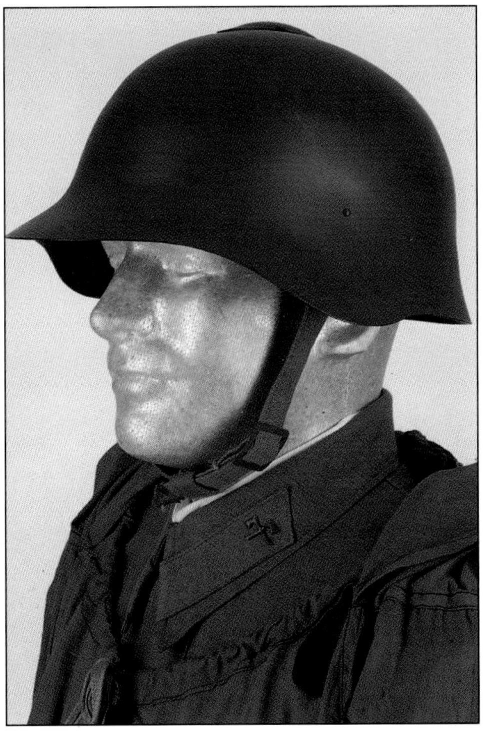

Army Private of Cavalry. Black buttons were used less frequently in the late 1930s and indicate this tunic is an early model.

Dark blue collar tabs with black piping were the cavalry colors.

Military Affairs and Intelligence winter field dress. This quilted jacket called a Telogreika was very popular for mild winter conditions. The gray cloth pouches are intended for Tokarev rifle magazines.

CHAPTER FOUR

1943-1945

As the Soviet Union fought the war, national sentiment for traditional values brought a return of pre-Revolutionary uniforms and insignia in January 1943. Traditional styles were adopted for all branches of the military. The shoulder board of the Czarist regime was brought back as a symbol of rank. The stand up collar and uniform colors of Imperial Russia were returned as regulation for the remainder of the war.

Marshal of the Soviet Union service and field dress. This tunic with standing collar was adopted January 1943 for officers of all services.

General Officer buttons with ribbons that signify the eleven Republics.

Marshal of Soviet Union shoulder board pattern adopted February 4, 1943. A short lived pattern was similar with a large star only. The final form added the embroidered Seal of the Soviet Union.

Marshal of the Soviet Union summer service dress.

Shoulder boards for Marshal of the Soviet Union service dress.

Another example of Marshal of the Soviet Union with gray service dress.

Marshal of Air Force service dress. The service gray (1943) was worn although traditional brown was more common.

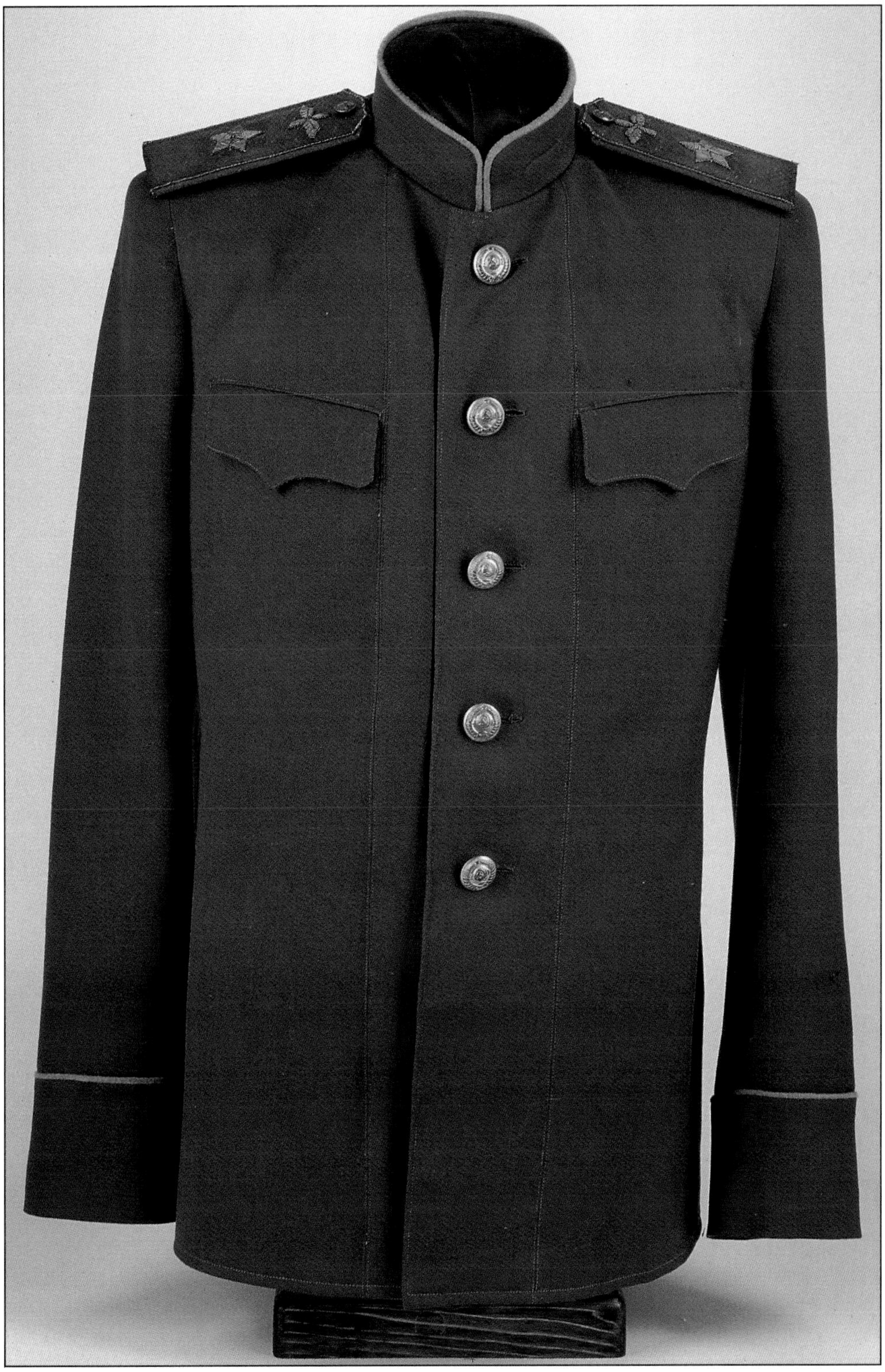

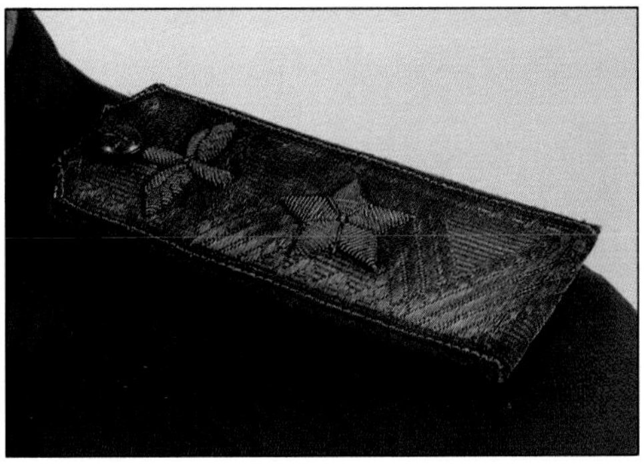

Shoulder board of the First Rank of Marshal used a single large star with the corps emblem.

Supreme Marshal of Armor service dress.

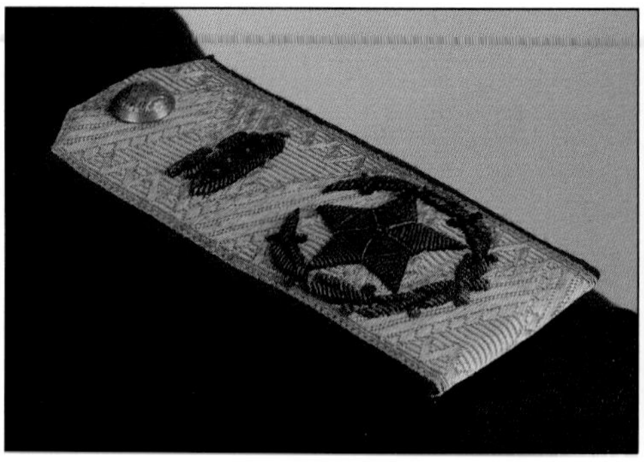

Supreme Marshal of Armor is one grade below Marshal of the Soviet Union. The rank was instituted October 27,1943.

Supreme Marshal of Artillery service dress. Artillery and Armor used the same colors for the visor cap.

Shoulder board for Supreme Marshal of Artillery.

Colonel General of the Army service dress.

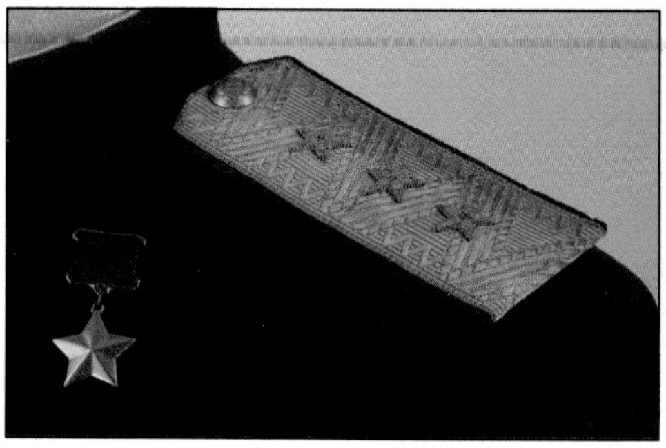

The same pattern shoulder board was used for rank of Colonel General by Infantry, Artillery and Armor.

Lieutenant General of Army service dress. Ribbon bars instead of full size medals became popular in 1944. Many soldiers and officers had received multiple decorations during the war years so the small ribbon representing each decoration was a convenient alternative.

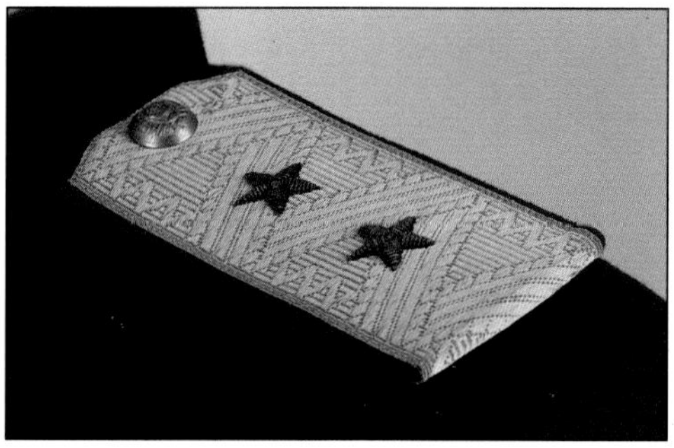

Lieutenant General service dress shoulder boards.

Major General of Army alternative service dress. The gray uniform was used by Generals for official functions. Film footage shows both gray and traditional brown worn at the same time.

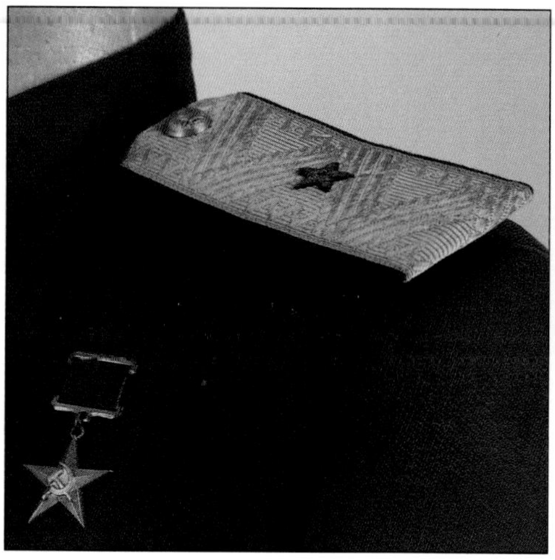

Major General shoulder boards on alternative gray service dress uniform.

Lieutenant General of Army summer service dress. This fabric was used frequently for high ranking personnel. Close inspection shows this the fabric is made using multi-colored fibers in the weave, giving the "salt and pepper" appearance.

Silver shoulder boards and chin cords were worn by Technical Generals.

Topcoat worn by General Officers. The buttons were "General" type with eleven Republics. The red tab on the collar indicates Infantry.

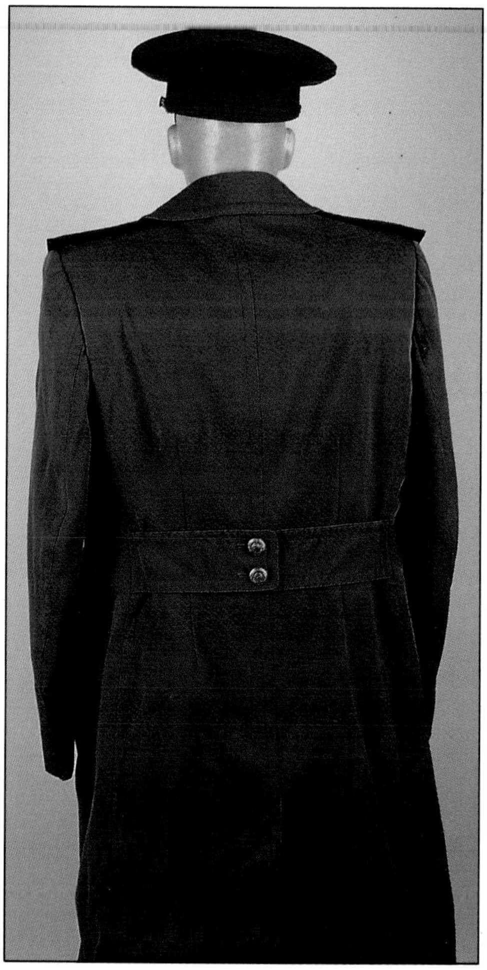

Back view of General Officers top coat.

Army Lieutenant General Official dress. This cap, worn with the standard service tunic, was usually reserved for non formal events.

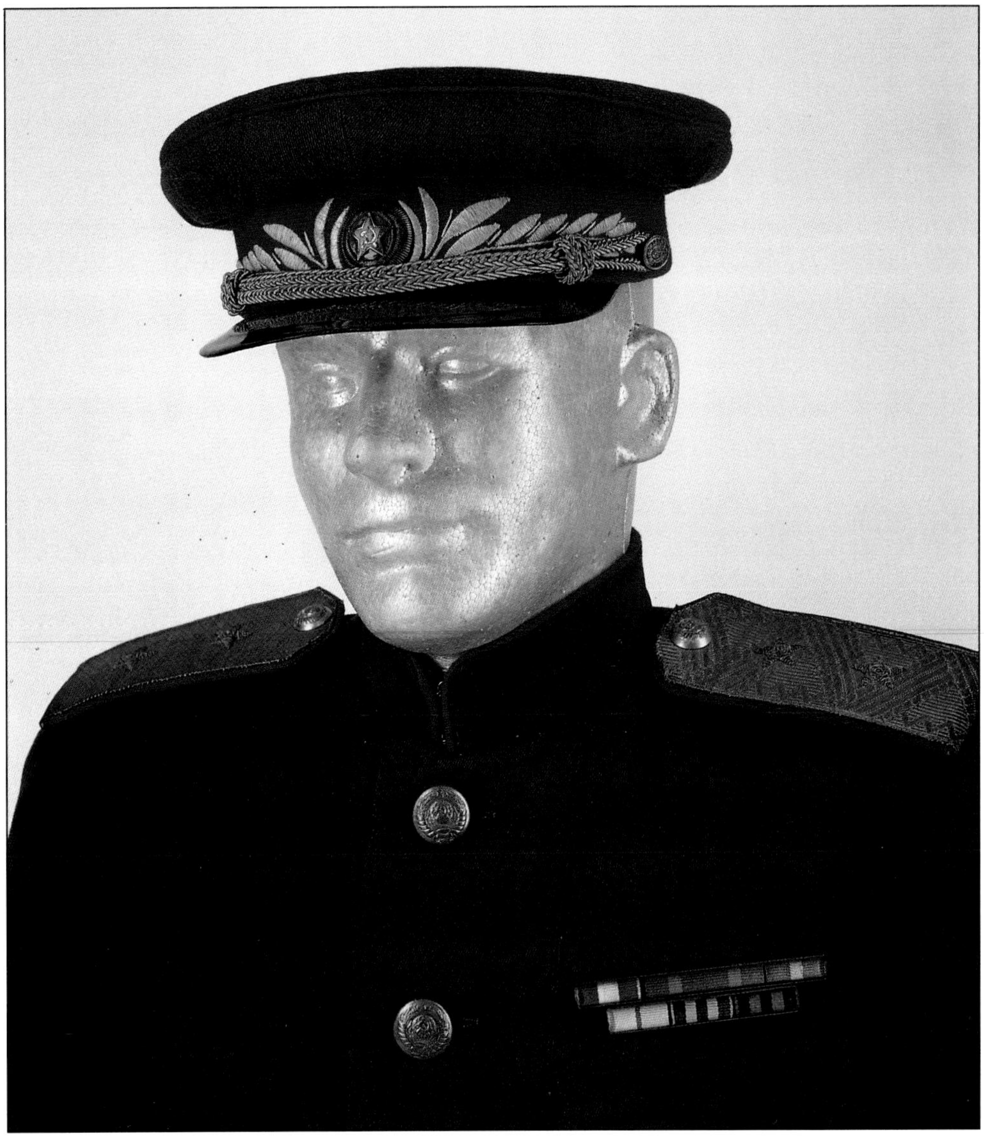

Major General Army field service. The fabric is a heavy rough wool intended for use without a greatcoat. The regular service cap was frequently used as a field cap. Decorations were worn in the field by many Generals and officers.

General Officer subdued field shoulder board. Metallic thread was not used for the decorative weave.

The General in the center of photo is not wearing Model 1940 General insignia on his visor cap.

NKVD Major General, circa 1945.

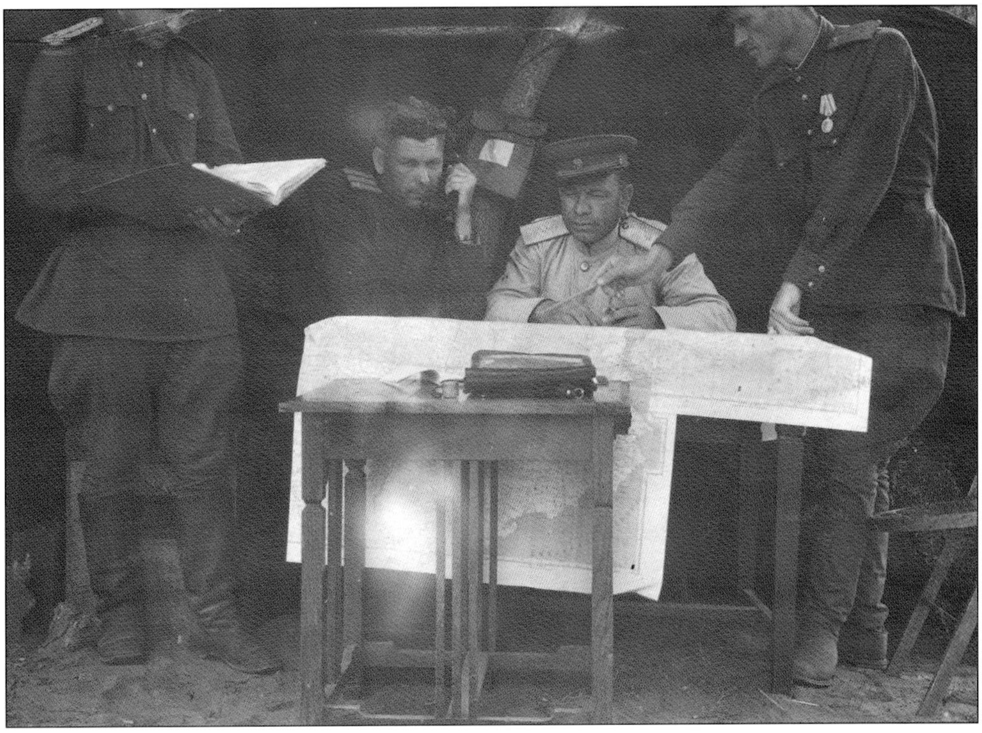

A general and staff in the field. The general is wearing a summer tunic.

Major General Army field service tunic without decorations and visor cap with no branch color. This style cap was worn extensively in the field.

Major General field service shoulder board. These shoulder boards, the "soft" type, have no hard interior for shape.

Naval Major General of Land Forces. The title Admiral was reserved for command personnel of sea going forces.

Sleeve rank insignia and these shoulder boards were worn only by command personnel of sea going forces.

Naval Frontier Troops General, pattern introduced in 1940. In 1943 shoulder boards were added and the sleeve rank was removed.

Naval Parade General, 1940/43. *(Photos this page by Les Kirby)*

Naval Major General Medical. Silver buttons and insignia were used on both tunics and visor caps for this branch of service.

Shoulder board for Naval Major General with Medical Branch insignia.

Air Force Major General with blue piping.

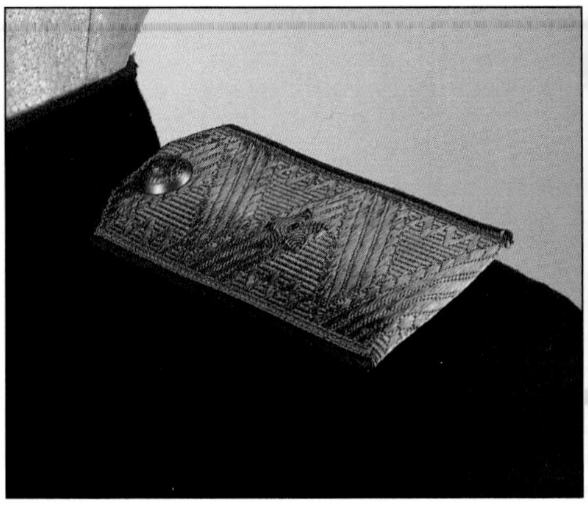

Air Force Major General. Senior Air Force ranks below Marshal did not wear branch insignia on shoulder boards.

Major General of Artillery. The black cap band was used by both Armor and Artillery to denote their branch.

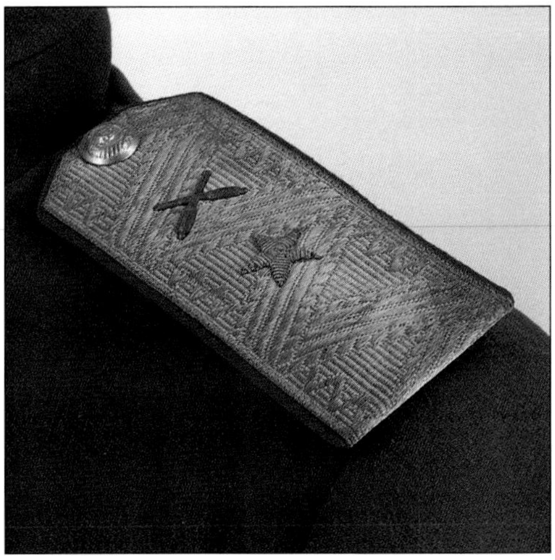

Major General of Artillery shoulder boards.

Marshal of Soviet Union parade uniform instituted January 15,1943.

Back view of Model 1943 parade uniform.

This collar was used only by Marshal of Soviet Union. Generals and Marshals of the branches wore a more delicate embroidery design. The Model 1945 parade uniform kept the collar and cuff design from the Model 1943 parade uniform.

Cuff detail of Marshal of Soviet Union parade uniform.

Air Force Major parade dress instituted January 25,1943.

Field Grade Officers (Major to General) used the double bar insignia on collar tabs.

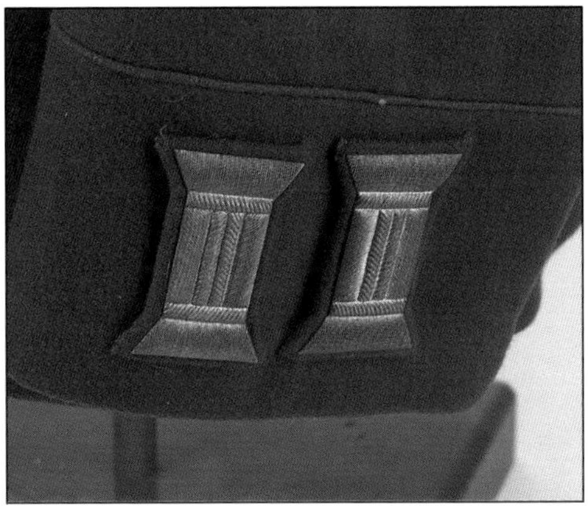

Two "spools" were worn on the cuffs by Field Grade Officers.

Greatcoat for Army General. The extensive use of colored piping first appeared in 1940. Addition of shoulder boards and changes to collar tabs upgraded this Greatcoat to 1943 regulations.

Back view of Generals Greatcoat.

Model 1943 collar tab and shoulder board.

Navy Captain 2nd Rank service uniform.

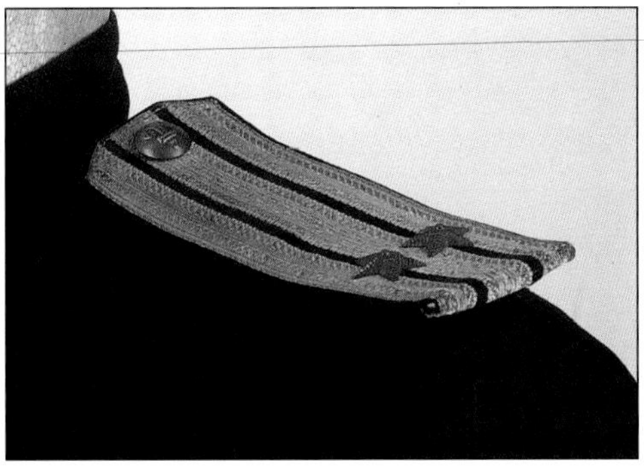

Shoulder boards and sleeve insignia were worn by sea going Command Personnel. Captain 1st Rank had three stripes on the shoulder board.

Sleeve stripes for Captain 1st and 2nd Ranks were the same. Prior to 1943, the sleeve stripes were sewn directly to the sleeve and ran from seam to seam. In 1943 shorter stripes were sewn to patch cloth and then to the uniform. The 1943 sleeve insignia was regulation for sea going command personnel. All others used shoulder straps only.

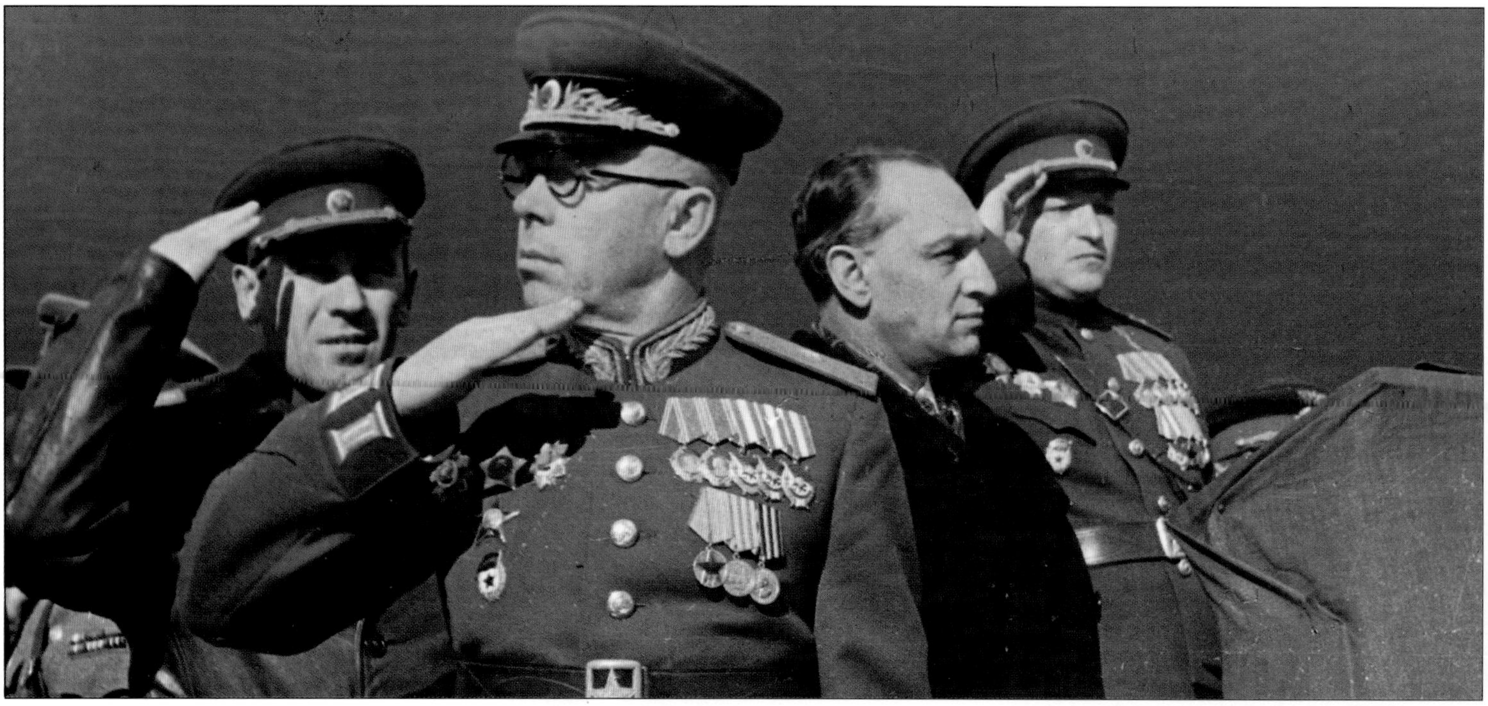

Above: Model 1943 gray parade dress Generals uniform worn with a 1940 pattern leather belt. A General wore three "spools" on each cuff with this pattern uniform.

Right: Diplomatic Corps Senior Official, 1945.

Right: Naval Officers and Petty Officers.

Navy Captain 2nd Rank parade dress. The Victory Parade in 1945 marked the first mass use of this new pattern uniform. Wearing medals and brocade belts was regulation.

Gold insignia was used for sea going Line Officers.

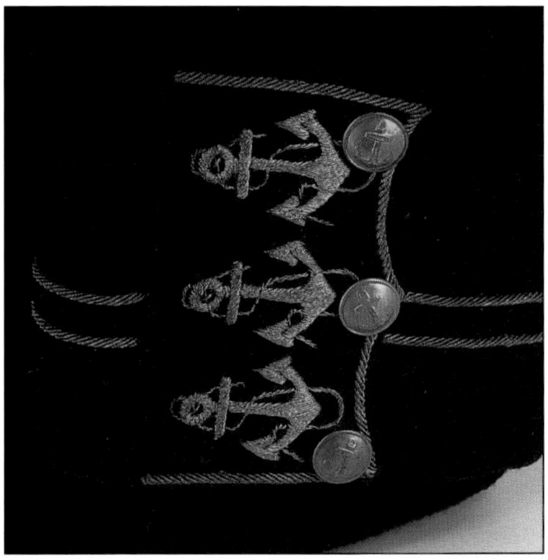

Anchor devices were worn with this pattern uniform to indicate Line Officer status. The anchors are seen in bullion metallic embroidery or stamped and gilded metal. Other branches used "spools " to denote status.

Marshal of Soviet Union parade uniform instituted in 1945. This uniform replaced the gray parade dress uniform of 1943. The pattern and color were inspired from Imperial uniforms. The color, czarist green, was given the name wave green by the Soviets. The brocade belt was in use until the Victory over Japan parade. At that time the vertical brocade piece was replaced with a buckle bearing the Seal of the Soviet Union.

The 1943 pattern embroidery on the collar tabs for the Marshal of the Soviet Union remained the same when changes were made in 1945.

The 1943 cuff pattern remained the same when 1945 changes were made.

Chief Marshal Engineering.

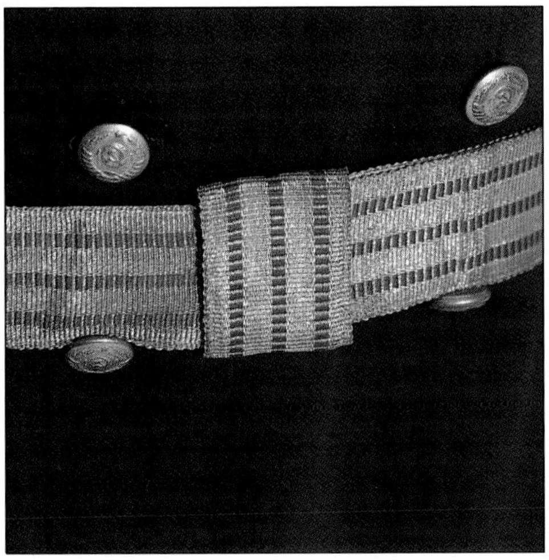

Parade belt of Engineering General Branch with raspberry branch color. *(Photos this page by Les Kirby)*

Insignia of Chief Marshal of Engineering.

Army Lieutenant General parade dress Model 1945. This brocade belt replaced the first pattern belt with the vertical closure.

Back view of Army General parade uniform.

Army General parade.

Army General parade.

1945 pattern Navy Admiral parade uniform.

Sea going Admirals used gold insignia. *(Photos this page by Les Kirby)*

Officers of the Line used anchors rather than spool device to signify rank.

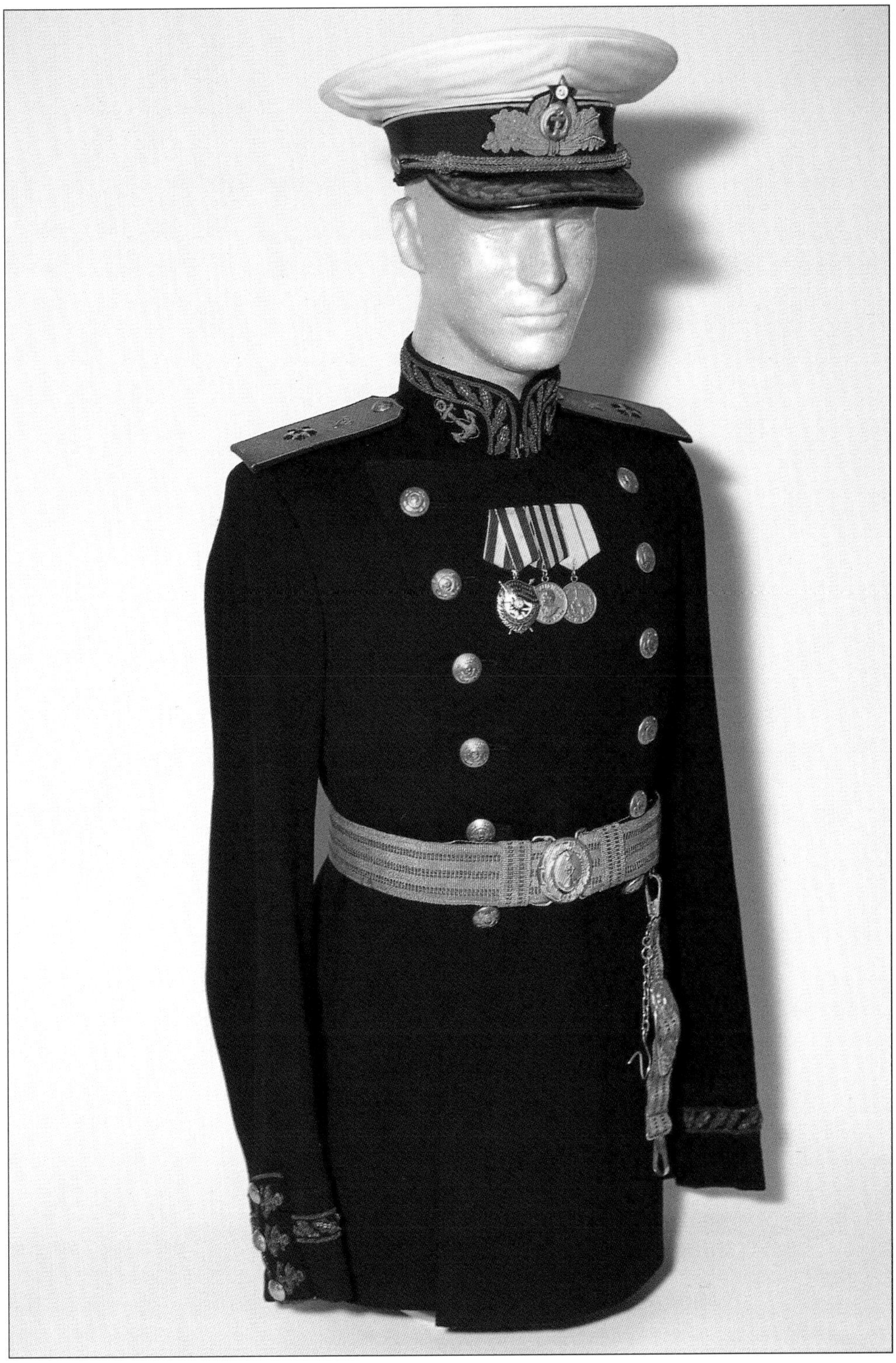

Naval Infantry General parade uniform, 1945.

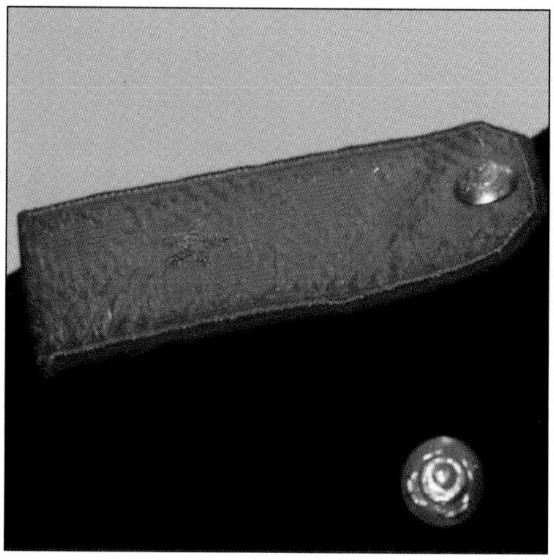

Naval Infantry branch color. *(Photos this page by Les Kirby)*

Naval Infantry Parade cuff.

Right: Officers of the Line, 1945.

Admiral parade uniform, 1945.

Right: Army Officers parade dress, 1945.

A Major General from 1943 to victory over Japan.

Naval General of Technical Engineering uniform. Leaf embroidery on the collar and cuffs denotes naval rank of Admiral and General.

Back view of Naval Officer and flag ranks parade tunic.

Sleeve detail of Naval General parade tunic.

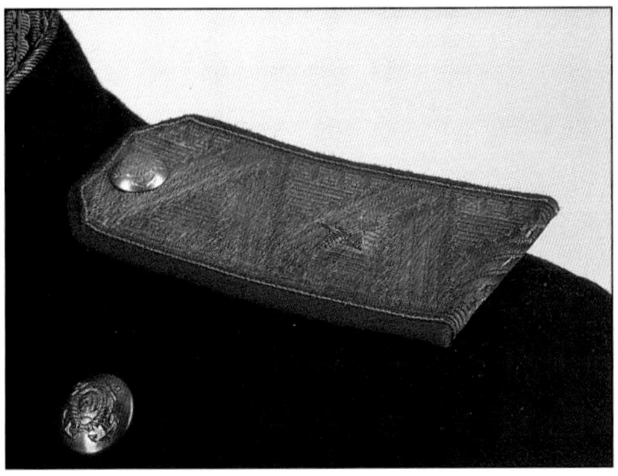

Shoulder board of Naval Major General with detail of buttons for flag ranks. The center is the Seal of the Soviet Union.

1945 Air Force General Officer parade dress uniform.

Air Force tunic and shoulder boards with light blue piping. *(Photos this page by Les Kirby)*

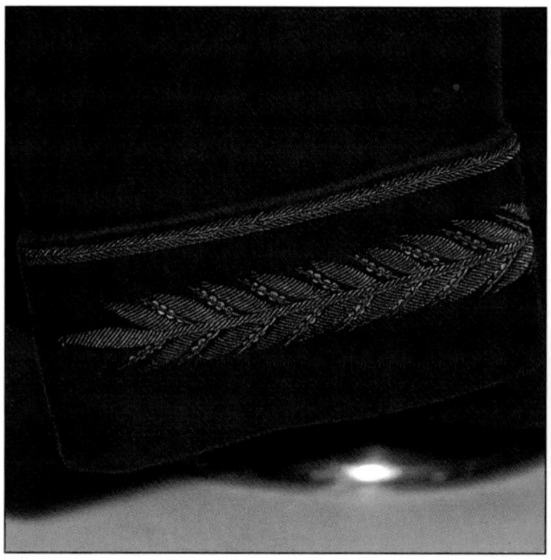

Detail of cuff, Air Force General.

Army Lieutenant Colonel Artillery parade dress Model 1943. The addition of collar tabs, sleeve insignia and piping on the front edging and back flaps of the 1943 service tunic, or Kitel, made it the officer's parade tunic. The two prong leather belt was regulation for parade dress, however the Model 1935 belt with the star buckle was also worn.

Back view of Army Officer parade tunic.

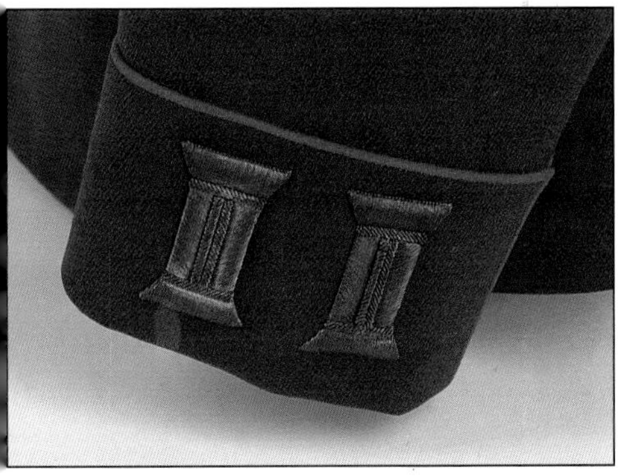

Cuff detail of field grade Officer. The two spools were used to denote the rank. On this example, the spools were directly embroidered to the cuff.

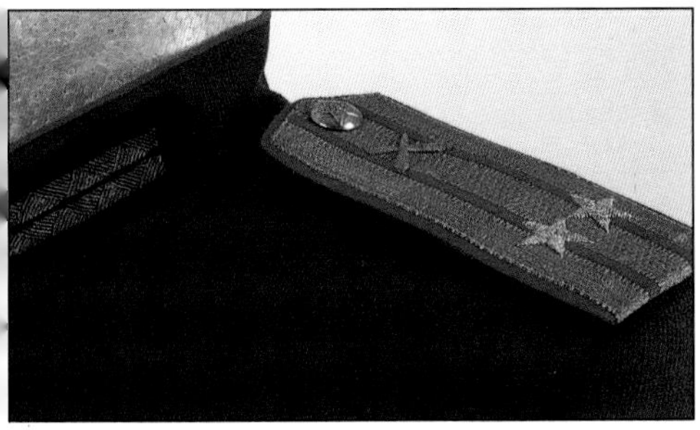

Lieutenant Colonel of Artillery shoulder boards.

Army General parade uniform 1945. Bullion work is done by hand and will vary slightly in size and style.

Major General parade uniform.

Cuff detail of General Officer parade tunic.

Right: Parade dress. Photo dated March 3,1946.

Major General parade dress. Special tailoring made the button easy to remove for the medal brace.

Right: A well fed Army General and his wife, 1945.

Army Major General of Engineers. General Officers and Marshals of Engineers used raspberry as their branch color.

Shoulder board Major General parade uniform.

Cuff of General Officer parade tunic. This one is General of engineers.

Army Major General parade dress of Technical Troops. Silver insignia for dress and parade dress was worn by branches such as Legal, Medical, Veterinary, and Supply.

Shoulder board Major General parade uniform Legal branch.

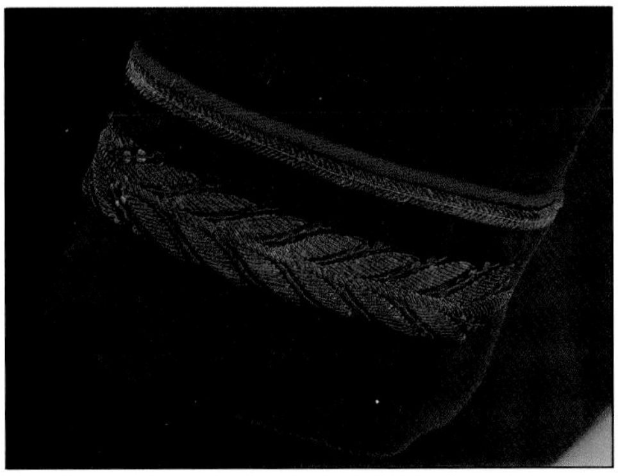

Cuff detail of General Officer parade tunic technical branch.

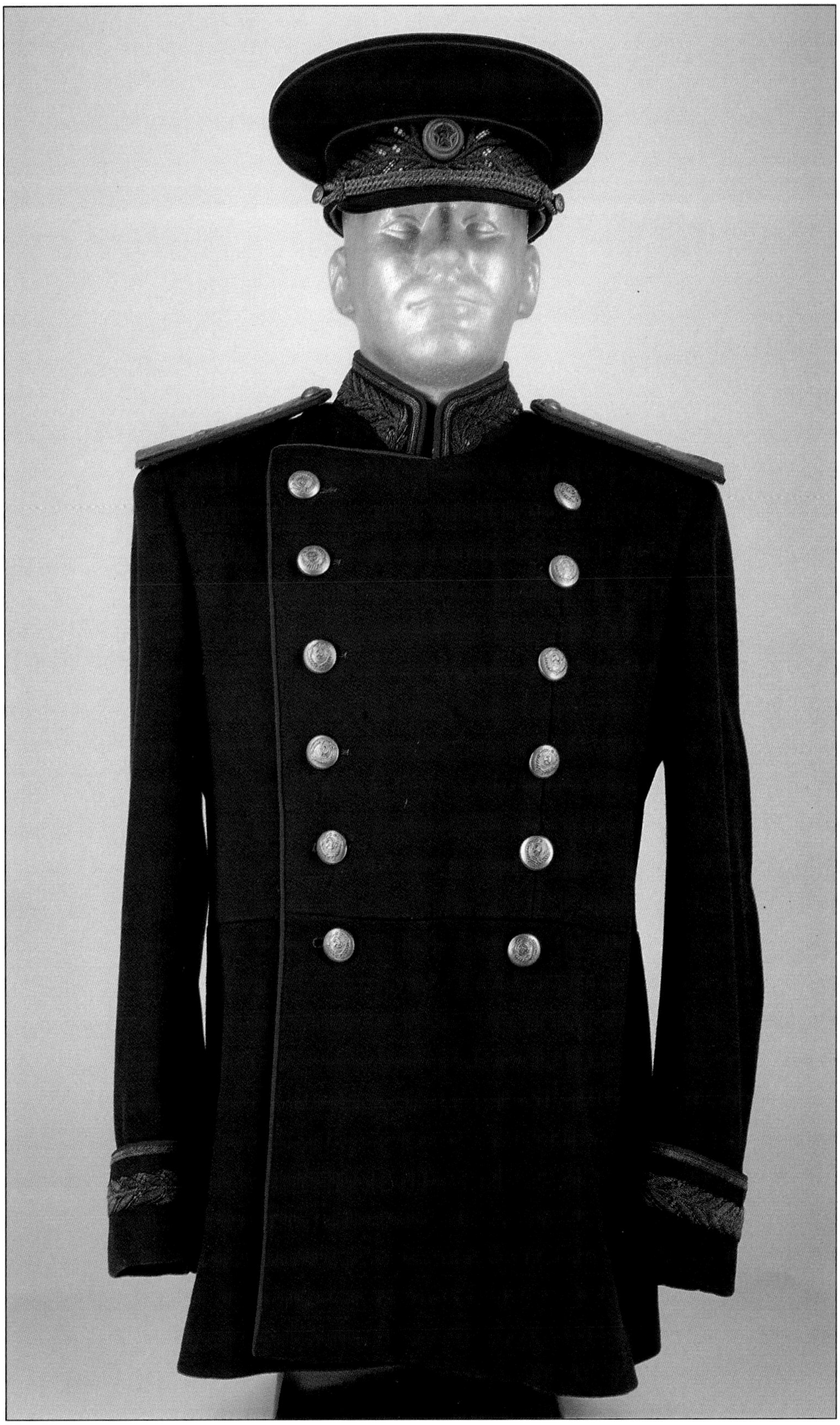

Naval Captain 1st Rank parade dress. Silver insignia was used by Medical branches.

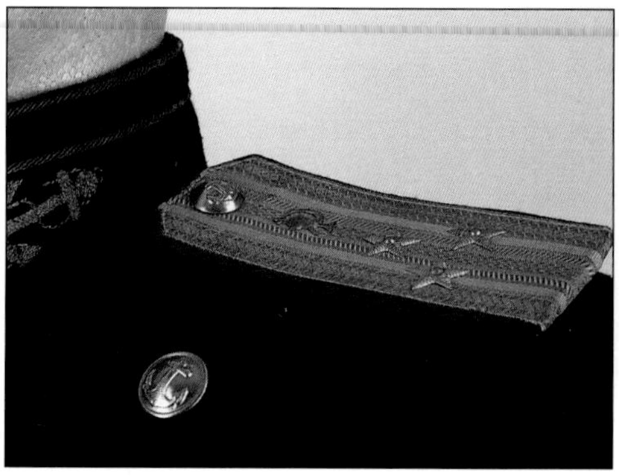

Shoulder board Captain 1st Rank Medical branch.

Three spools on the cuff denote Senior Rank. This photo shows detail of spools that were stamped metal rather than embroidered.

Army Sergeant of Armor parade dress 1945.

The collar tab for sergeant had a gold or silver strip. A soldiers collar tabs would be plain cloth in the branch colors.

Army Lieutenant of Infantry parade dress 1945.

A single bar in metal or bullion was the collar device for Junior Officers. The shoulder board had a single colored branch stripe through the center. Field Grade officers (Major and above) had two strips in branch colors.

A single spool of gilded metal or bullion was worn on the cuff of Junior Officers.

NKVD Frontier Troops or Border Guards Lieutenant parade dress.

The back view shows four buttons and the branch color piping.

The spool design was used rather than bars for Frontier troops.

Single spool on cuff for Junior Grade Officers.

Army Major of Artillery field service Gymnastiorka with high collar and shoulder boards introduced in January 1943 This example has brown plastic buttons made in the USA as part of the Lend-lease program. The map case is one of several patterns in use during the war.

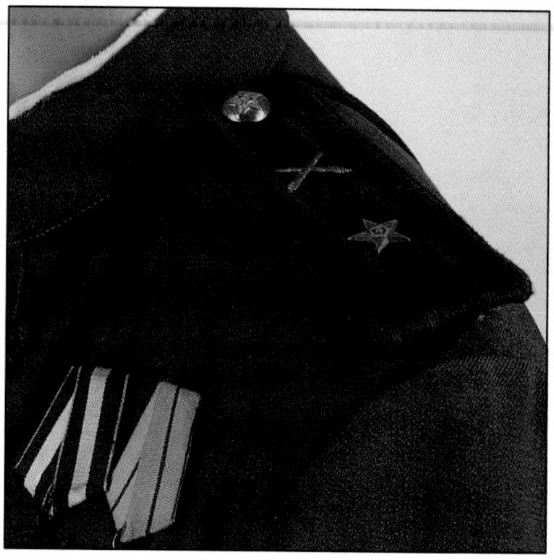

Field pattern Artillery Major shoulder boards. Note detail of white collar insert. A white cotton fabric was frequently hand tacked inside the collar on this style tunic.

Model 1943 parade dress Captain of Technical branch.

A well decorated Tank Officer, 1945.

At rest, 1944.

A group of Air Force Officers showing the wide variety of insignia worn in the field.

Right: Note the whistle pouch on the 1932 pattern field kit.

An officer with OD Field cap and a soldier with pocketless gymnastiorka.

Right: Four Army officers, circa 1944.

NKVD Major Frontier Troops or Border Guards field service. The same style Gymnastiorka was worn for service and field dress. Officers frequently adopted a darker color and higher quality fabric.

NKVD Frontier Troops Major shoulder boards.

Army Infantry Major service dress. This pattern tunic or Kitel was introduced January 1943. It was the replacement for the Model 1935 and 1940 tunics.

Shoulder boards Infantry Major service dress. The boards were not made with metallic thread.

Major General, summer white tunic.

Army General, Model 1943 summer white tunic.

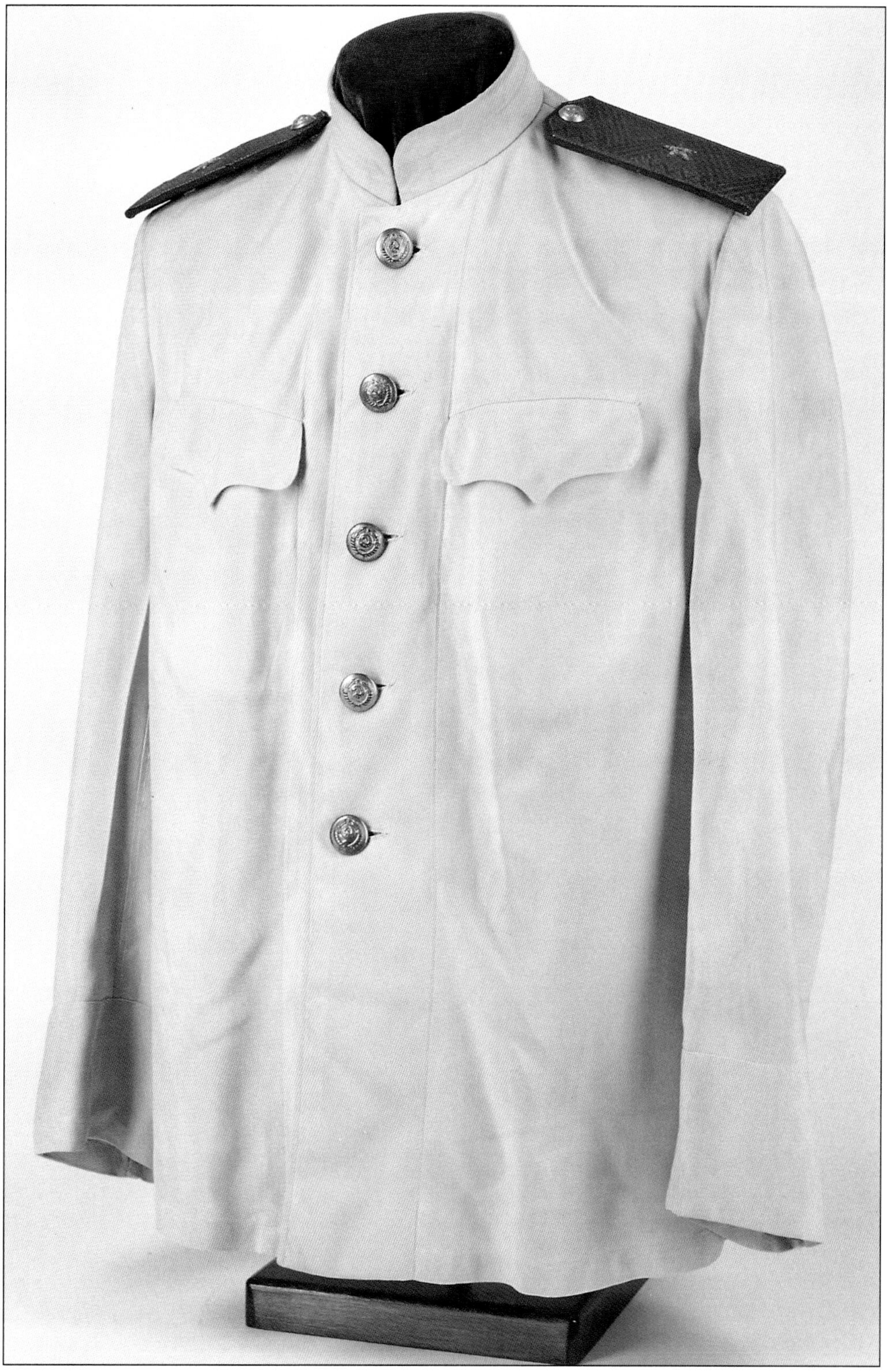

Army Captain, summer 1944.

This photo shows two unusual tunics. Both have exterior pockets and one has plain buttons.

Major, Model 1943 tunic. This variation has straight pocket flaps. Dated 1945.

Artillery officers, summer 1944.

Army Major of Artillery, summer white tunic.

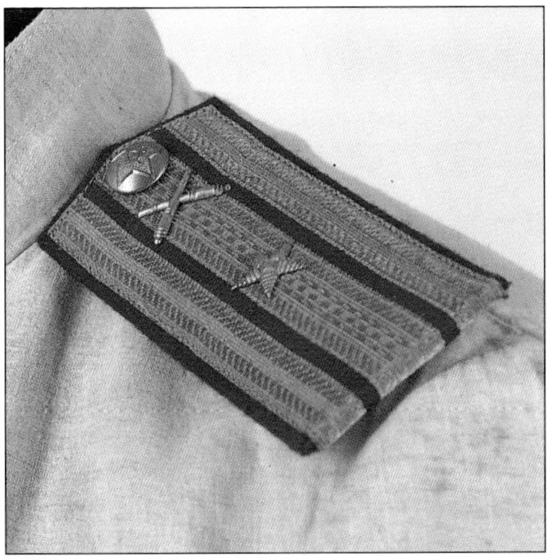

Artillery Major in summer white.

Army Junior Lieutenant Technical Troops parade dress Model 1943.

Shoulder board shows the single stripe and star of Junior Lieutenant.

Air Force Master Sergeant parade dress Model 1943.

Insignia of Master Sergeant shown on collar tabs.

Army 1st Sergeant of Artillery, parade dress Model 1943.

Insignia of 1st Sergeant.

Suvorov Military Academy parade dress.

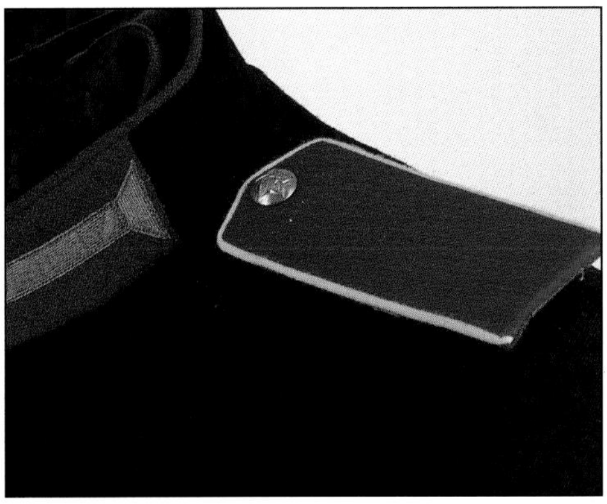

This collar tab was common to student ranks. These board colors represent the Suvorov Academies. High ranking students had metallic thread sewn around the inside edge of the shoulder board. School location was frequently embroidered on the boards.

Insignia of Cadet Sergeant.

The belt and buckle shown here were introduced for cadets. After the war a similar pattern was used for enlisted personnel throughout the army.

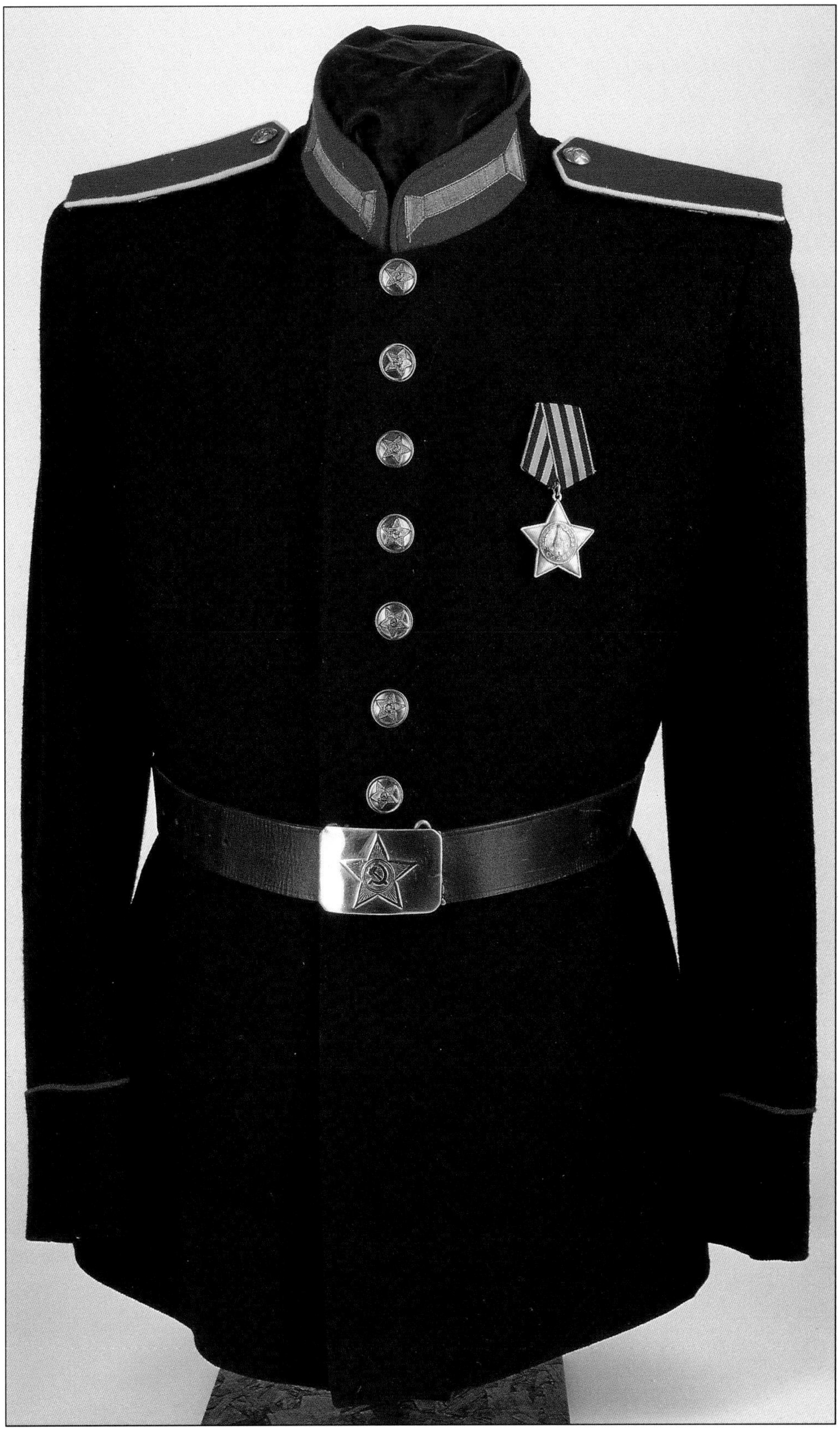

NKVD Senior Lieutenant service dress.

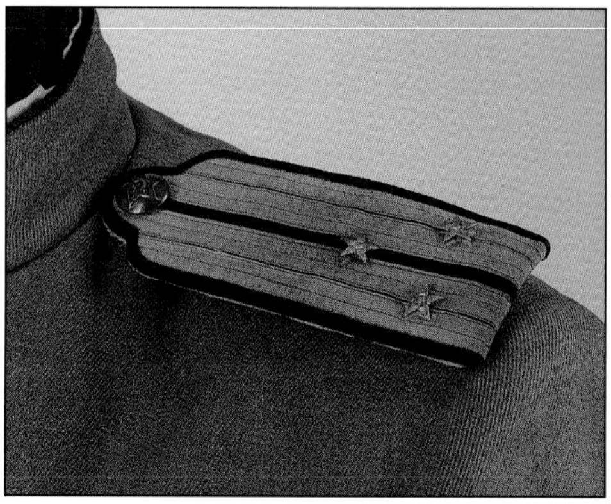

When shoulder boards became regulation, this unusual shoulder board was designed and worn by NKVD.

Army Colonel Technical Troops Women's service dress.

These metallic bullion stars are embroidered directly to the shoulder boards.

Air Force Master Sergeant.

Colonel of Armor. Staff and field grade officers wear larger stars on the shoulder straps. Photo dated 1943.

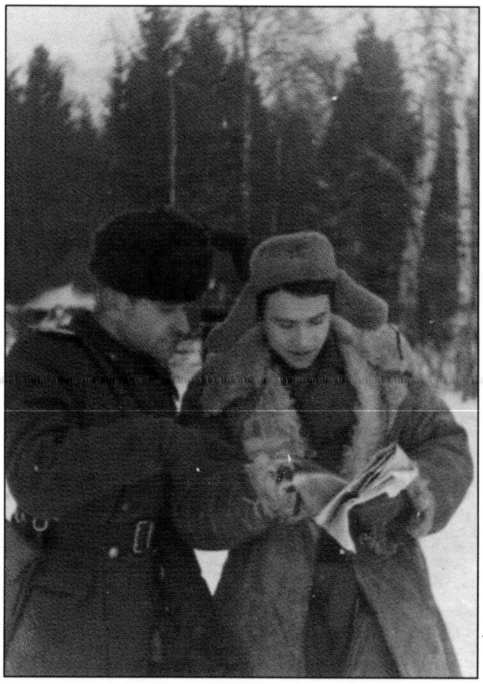

The soldier (right) is wearing a coat make entirely of sheepskin. Note holster without belt kit. Photo dated 1945.

These Officers are wearing the service dress shoulder board, circa 1945.

Tank crew in coveralls at their T-34.

Army Lieutenant Colonel of Engineers field service dress.

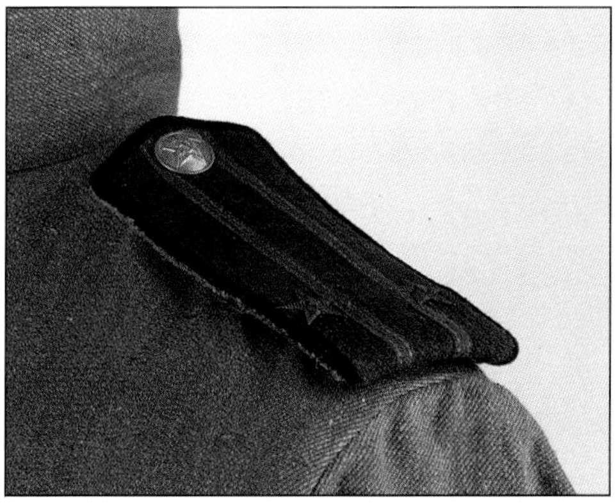
Subdued shoulder board of Lieutenant Colonel.

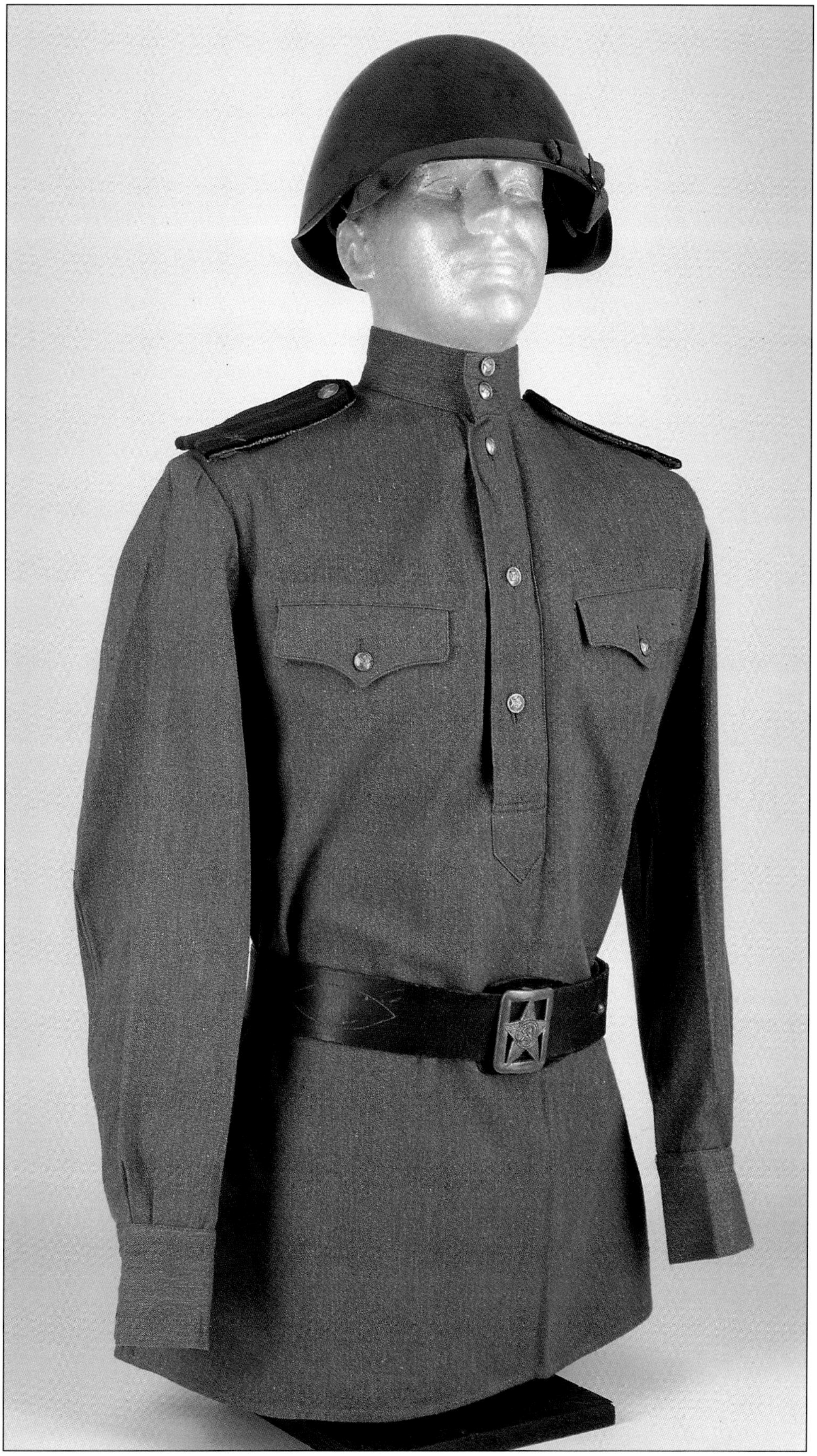

Army Officer Top Coat field dress.

Collar tabs worn on top coats indicated branch of service. These field pattern boards worn by a Captain are without corps devices.

Army Lieutenant Gymnastiorka. This tunic was reported to have been made in Leningrad during the siege. The buttons are cast lead dipped in black paint.

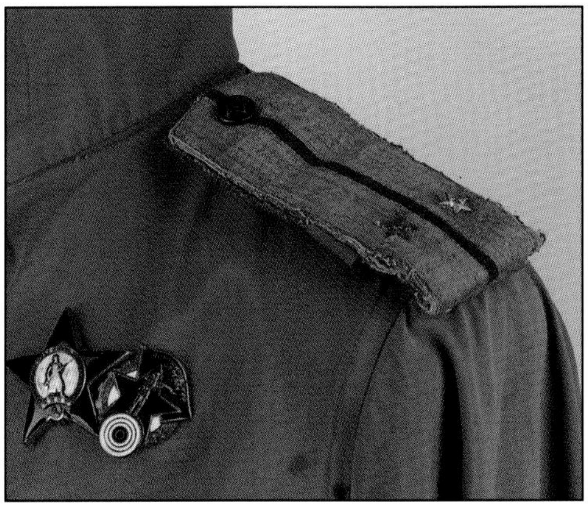

The tress used to make these shoulder boards was made from surplus czarist stock.

Army Major of Armor, service dress. Pre-1943 armor headgear was frequently worn with the Model 1943 uniform. After January 1943 regulation headgear was the same for Armor and Artillery personnel.

Service Board worn on Gymnastiorka.

Army Captain of Artillery field dress uniform.

Captain field insignia.

Naval Line Officer summer service uniform.

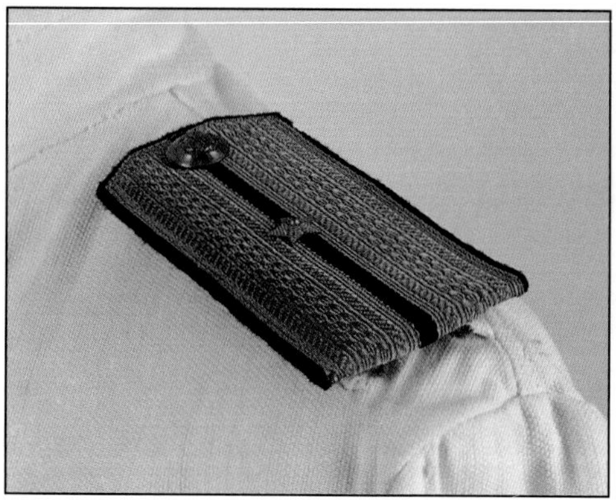

Insignia of Sub-lieutenant Line Officer.

Naval Technical Officer summer service.

Senior Lieutenant of Engineers.

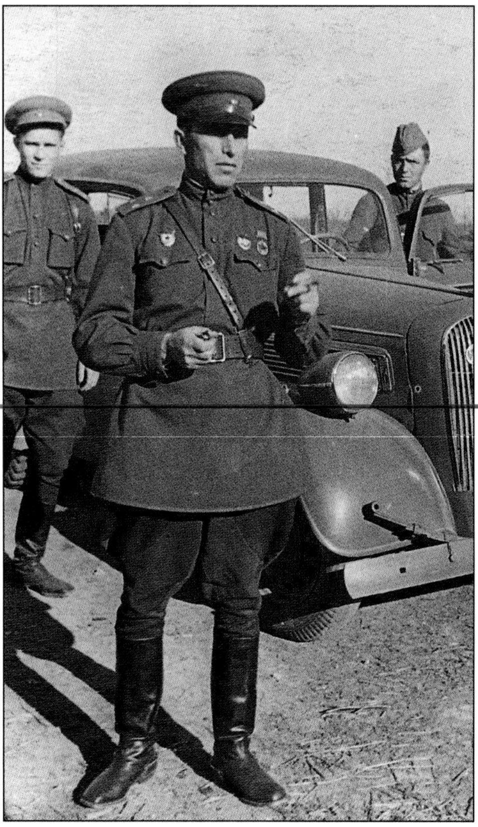

Infantry colonel with aides, 1944.

Six of these Officers are wearing the Model 1940 Shapka-Ushanka pile cap. The center officer is wearing the special astrakan hat for Colonels. Photo dated 1944.

Gymnastiorka with buttons made of stamped steel. They were used when regular buttons were unavailable. Photo dated 1944.

Troops in full winter gear, circa 1943.

Army Master Sergeant of Artillery service dress. The early pattern Gymnastiorka were worn with 1943 pattern insignia until supplies were available. The belt is from a German Officer. The Soviets often used captured German material.

Shoulder boards worn by Army Master Sergeant of Artillery service dress.

Army Junior Sergeant winter battle dress. The equipment consists of canvas grenade pouch and ammunition for the 7.65x54R. The combat knife, dated 1942, is a common example.

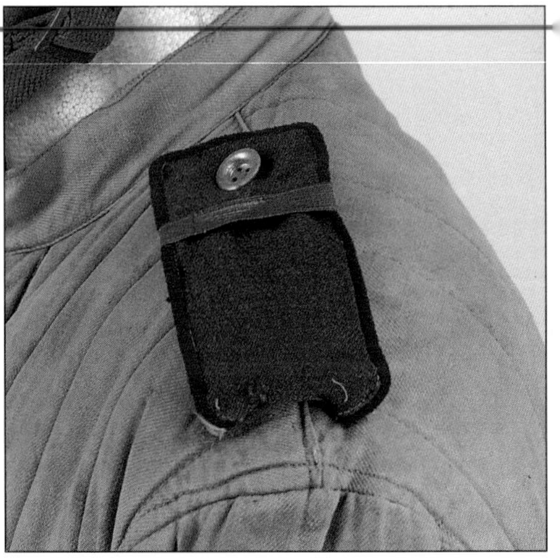

Shoulder board worn by Junior Sergeant, although shoulder boards were usually not worn on this pattern jacket by lower ranking personnel.

Interested Artillery Officers, 1944.

Youthful cadet. Photo dated 1945.

Post war photo of a well decorated officer. Wearing the uniform without rank insignia was common for deactivated personnel. Photo dated 1948.

Army Private with Model 1940 "fish fur" pile cap. The insignia worn on these caps varied in size and frequently no insignia was worn.

This multi-wounded soldier has very unusual accoutrements. The cross strap is German, the belt is likely American lend-lease, the leggings are German, and the star is a size usually worn on an overseas cap.

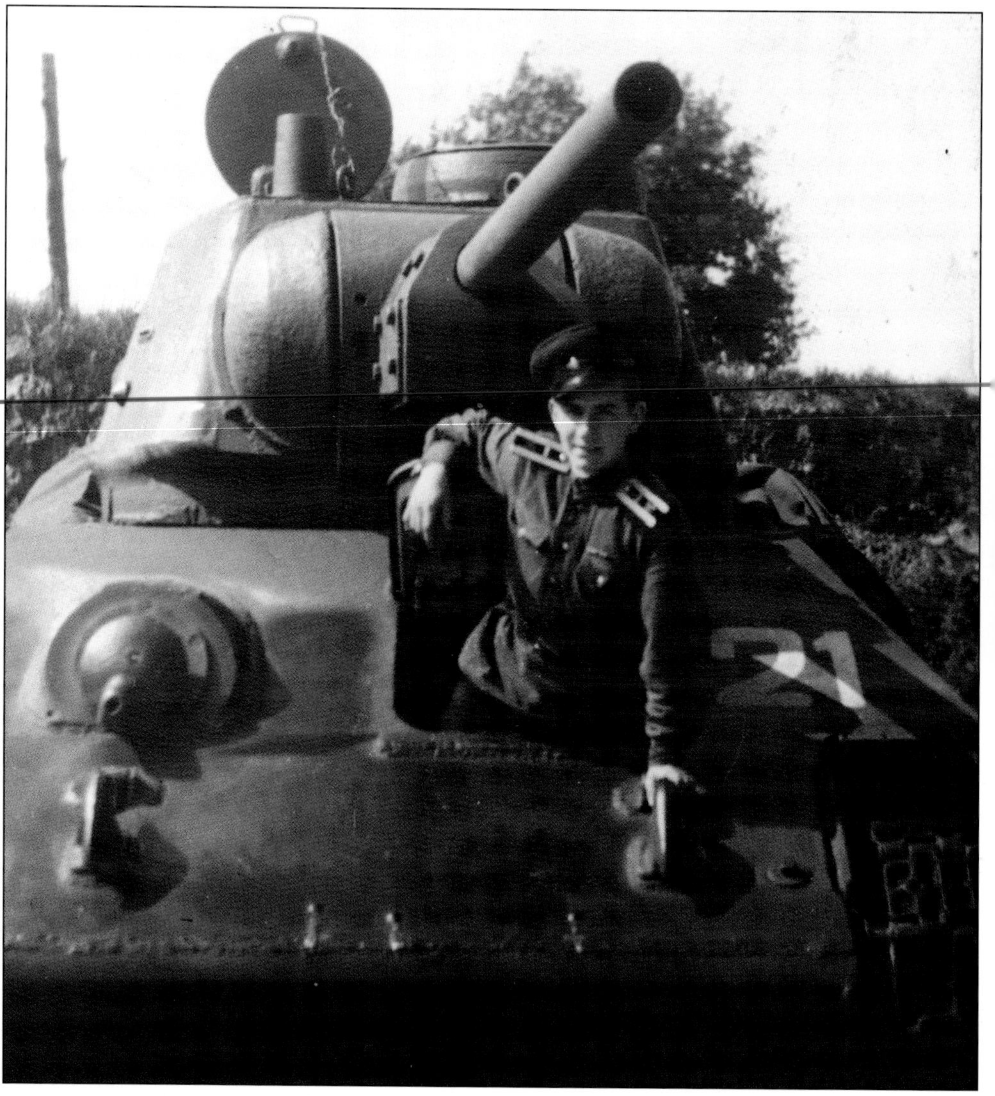

Right: Cadet of Armor troops, 1945.

Women soldiers in service dress, circa 1944.

Army Private service and field dress.

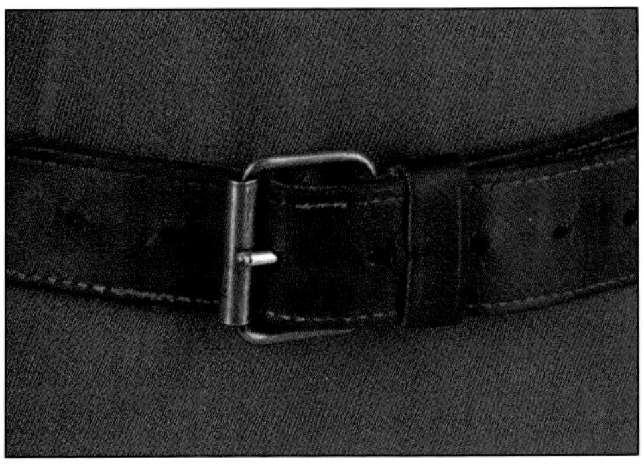

Enlisted mans leather belt.

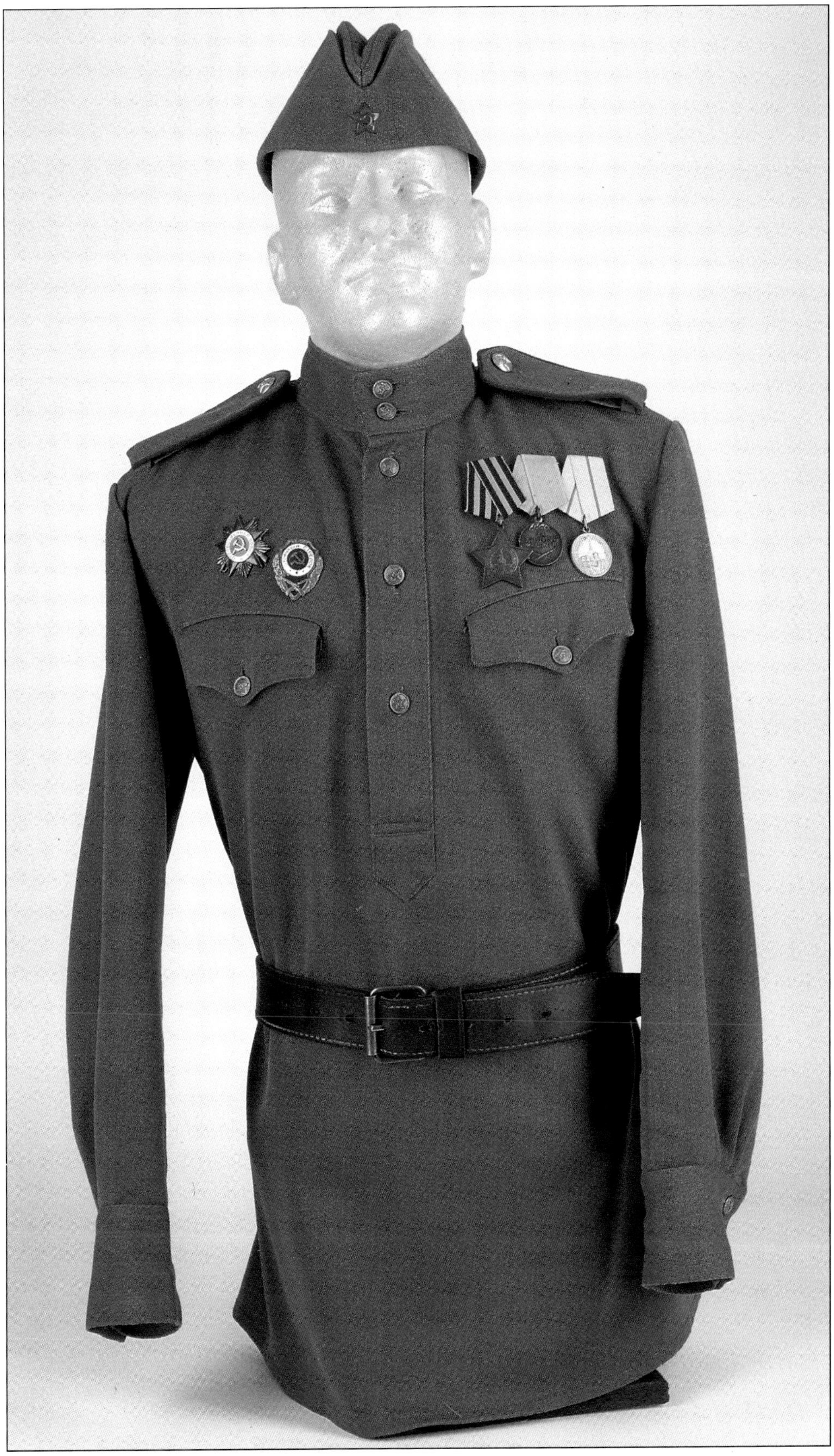

Army Private uniform produced in Leningrad during the siege.

Army Private field service. The red badge cloth worn over the pocket indicates a wound in battle.

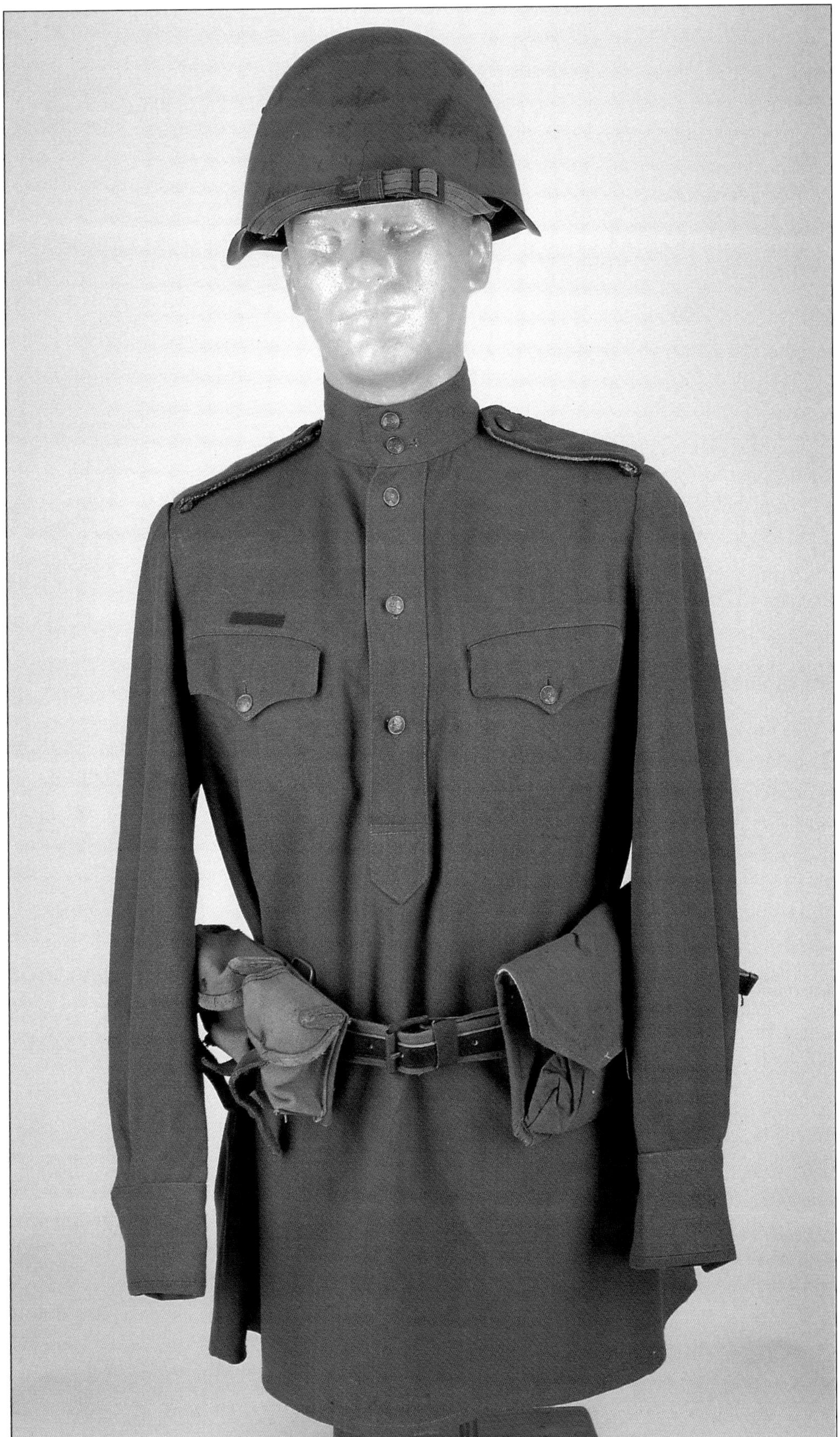

CHAPTER FIVE

Headgear

Like all Soviet militaria during this period, changes and improvements were being made to headgear on a continuing basis. More practical styles were introduced and many changes were made due to shortages of material during the war. Many regulation changes were not adopted in the field until current supplies were exhausted and new supplies arrived. As shown throughout this book, period photographs illustrate the resourcefulness and individuality of the men in the field.

The Adrian pattern helmet was manufactured and purchased under license from France. It was adopted by the Imperial Russian Army during World War I. During the 1920s and early 1930s many were upgraded and worn by the Soviets. Insignia varied, from stamped to painted insignia.

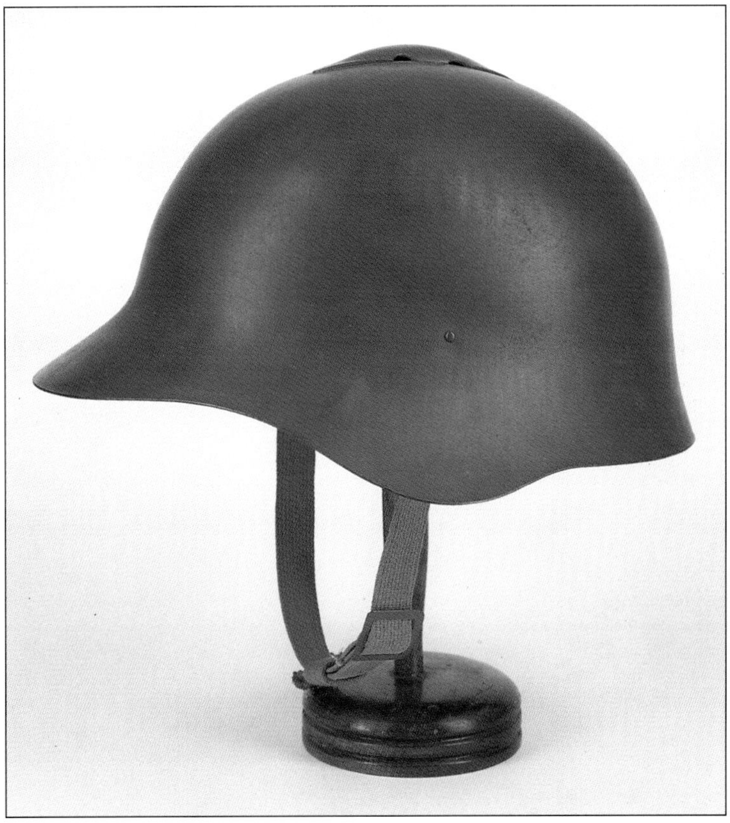

Model 1936 steel helmet. This design was made to replace the Imperial pattern Adrian helmet.

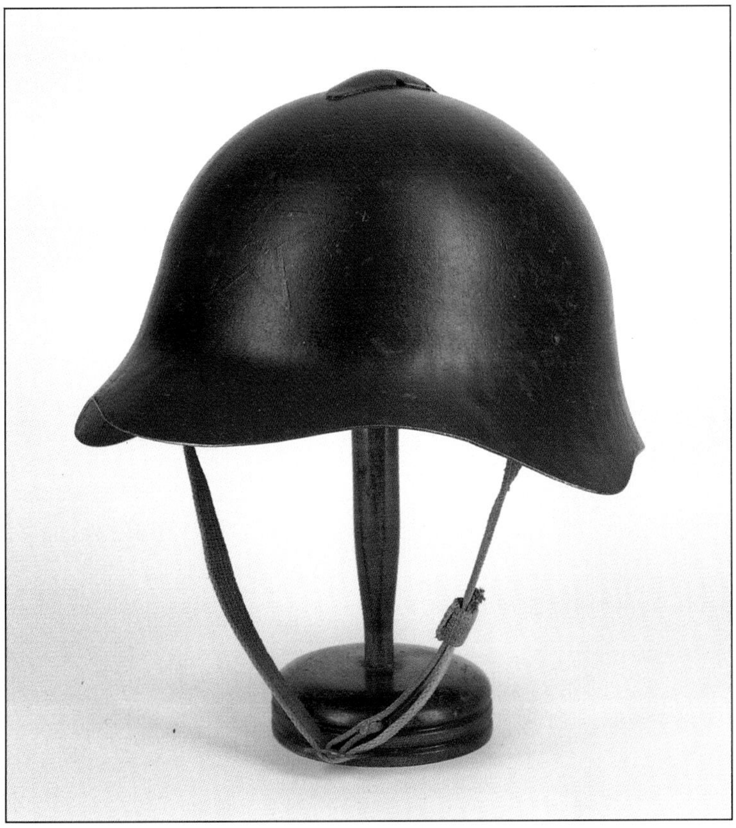

Model 1936 Helmet with red star. This insignia was adopted by many regiments.

Right: Interior of 1936 helmet. The first liner design was pieced together with a cloth spacer. Design and material were weak and liners would fall out after little use.

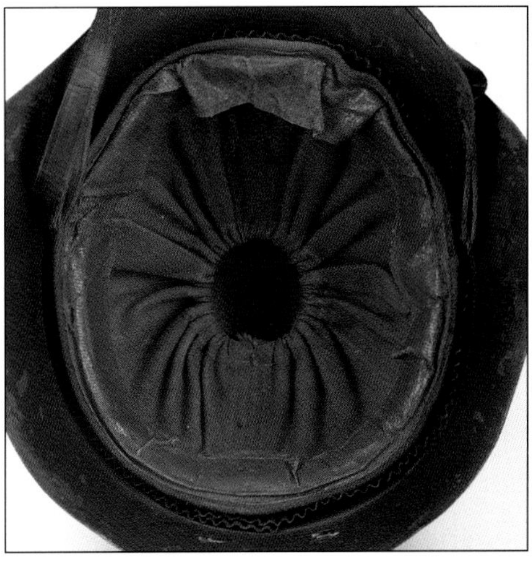

Right: Interior of 1936 helmet with improved liner. This liner was constructed with heavy canvas and artificial leather sweatband. The leather chin strap was later replaced with canvas.

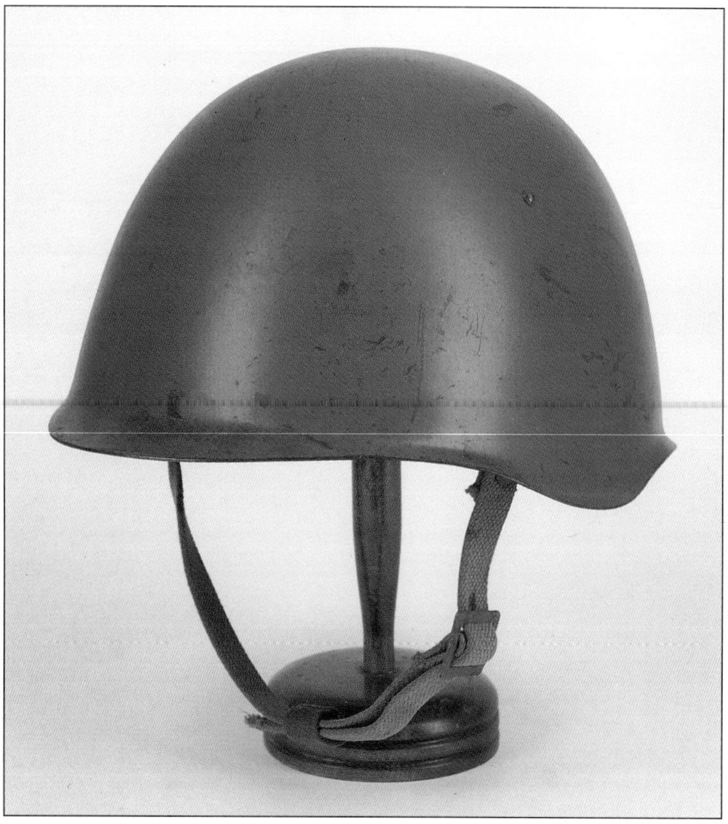

Model 1940 steel helmet. By this time the Model 1936 was seen as a less modern than helmets worn by the other super powers. This Model 1940 was an up to date design.

Right: Detail of markings and 1941 date on interior of helmet.

Right: Model 1940 steel helmet with first pattern liner.

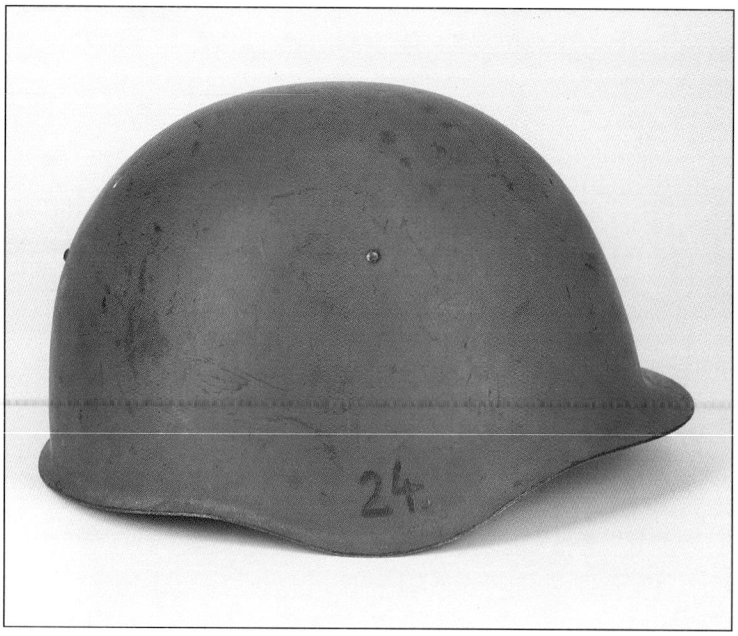

Profile of the Model 1940 helmet. Note the position of the rivet on the helmet shell. The later pattern 1936 liners were used in the new helmets until 1943.

Model 1940 helmet with later pattern liner. The rivets are in a lower position to accommodate the three pad liner. The solid red star is one variation used by regiments.

Model 1940 helmet later pattern.

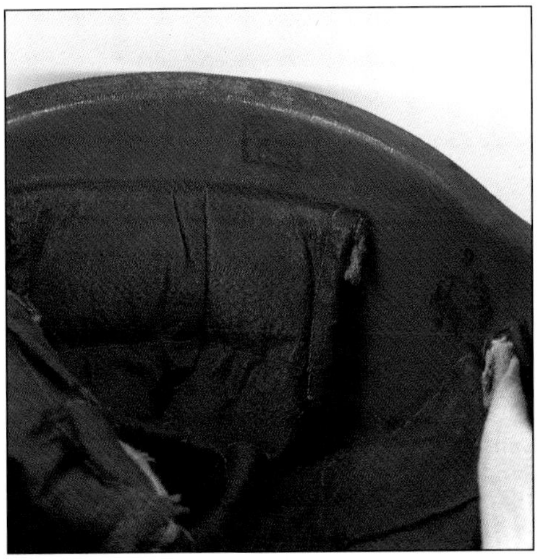

Right: Model 1940 helmet liner. Note the 1944 date.

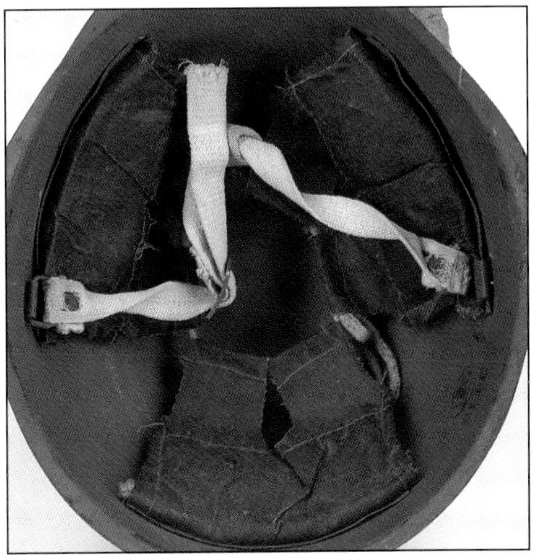

Right: Late pattern Model 1940 helmet with the three pad liner.

Fireman's helmet of wartime Russia.

Right and two photos at the top of page 220: Three NKVD Blocking Troops Budionovka. The two caps with the higher point are 1927 patterns and the shorter point is a 1935 pattern. The NKVD Blocking troops functioned as Military Police. The Term "Blocking" means preventing your troops from retreating from battlefield positions.

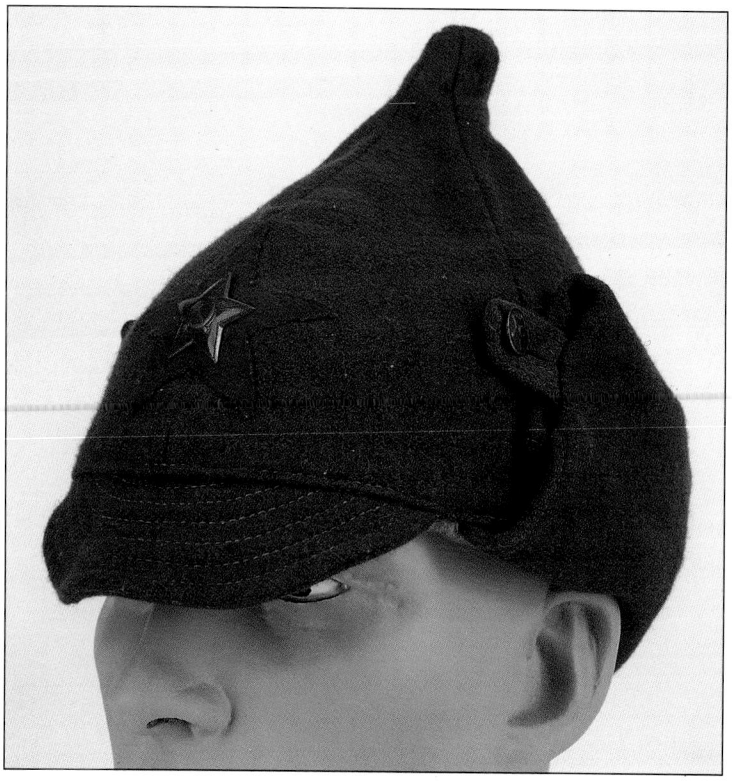

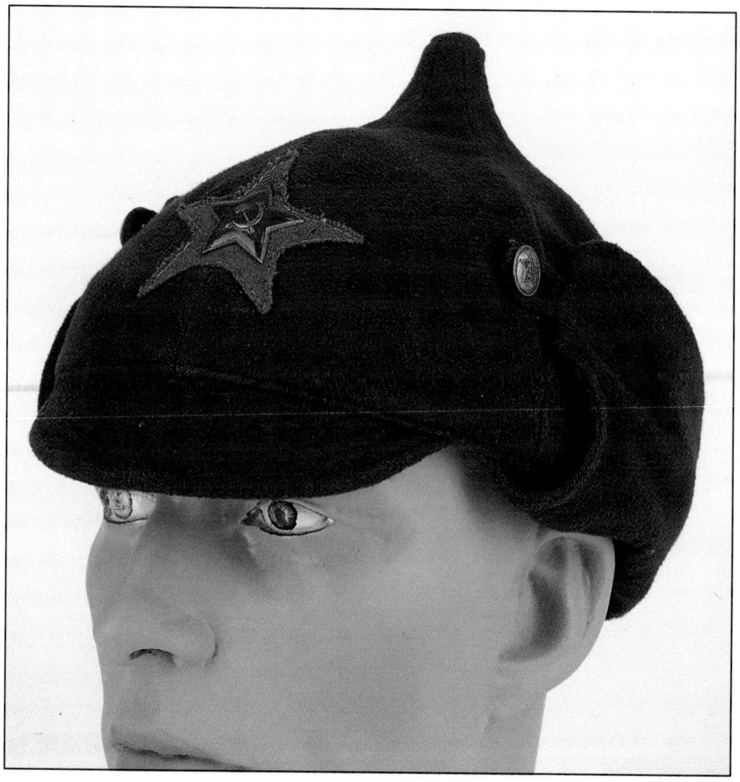

NKVD State Security Budionovka. The star is in brick red branch color.

Infantry Officer Budionovka with raspberry branch color star. The fabric is high quality and the metal and enamel star is in two pieces.

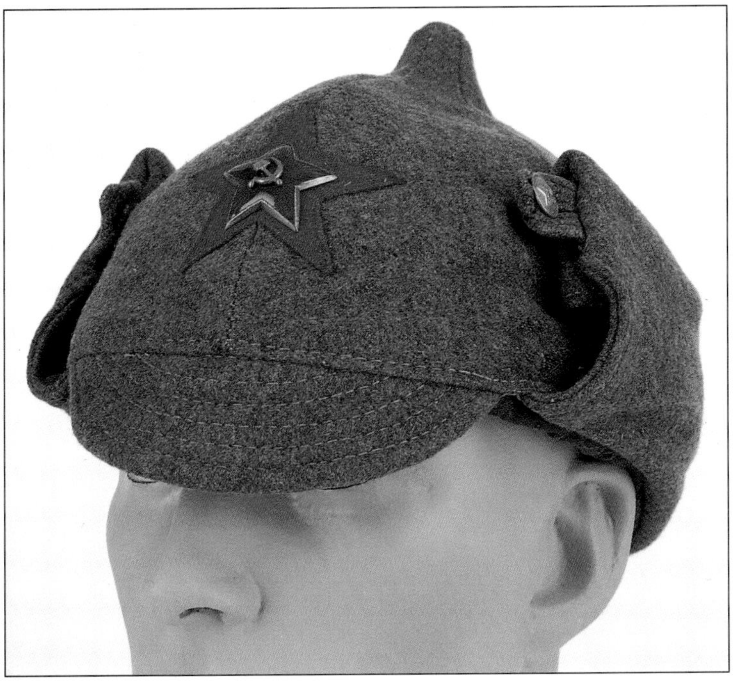

Infantry Enlisted Budionovka made with rough fabric and a one piece Model 1935 star.

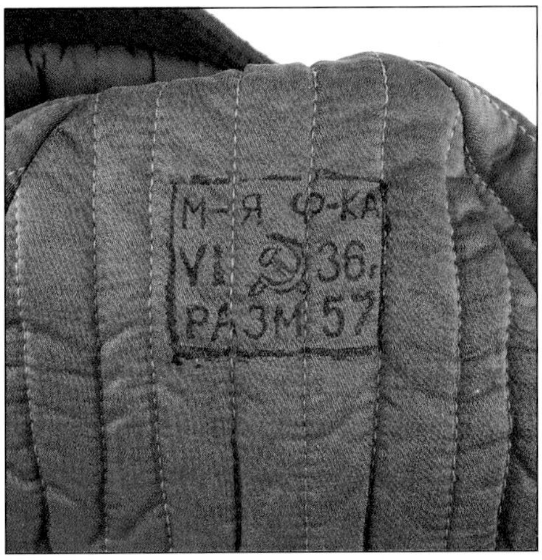

Right: Interior view of Infantry Officer Budionovka manufactured in 1936.

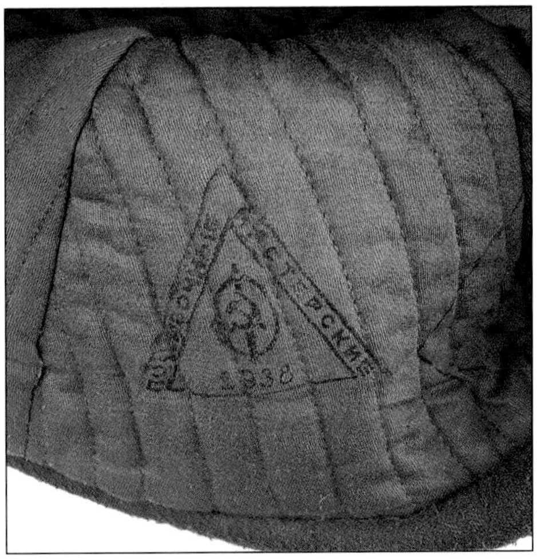

Right: Infantry Enlisted Budionovka with 1938 manufacture date.

Infantry Enlisted summer weight Budionovka made of a rough weave cotton.

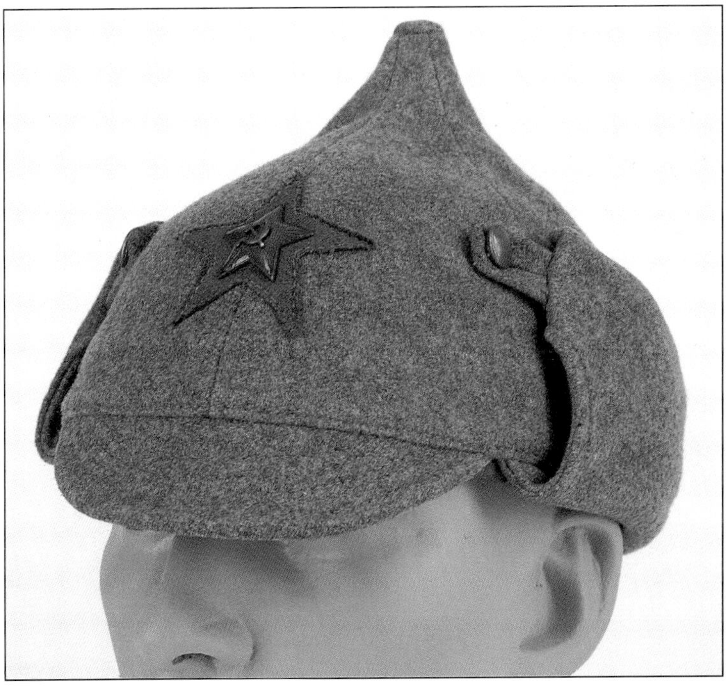

Air Force Officer of General Staff in gray and light blue, the distinctive colors of Air Force General Staff.

Armor Officer Budionovka. The black star and gray body indicate tank personnel. The large enamel and metal star is a 1935 Senior Commander pattern worn by many officers after the introduction of the Generals cap Insignia in 1940. Officers who had them wore them.

Armor Enlisted Man summer weight Budionovka.

Artillery Officer olive brown Budionovka with black star.

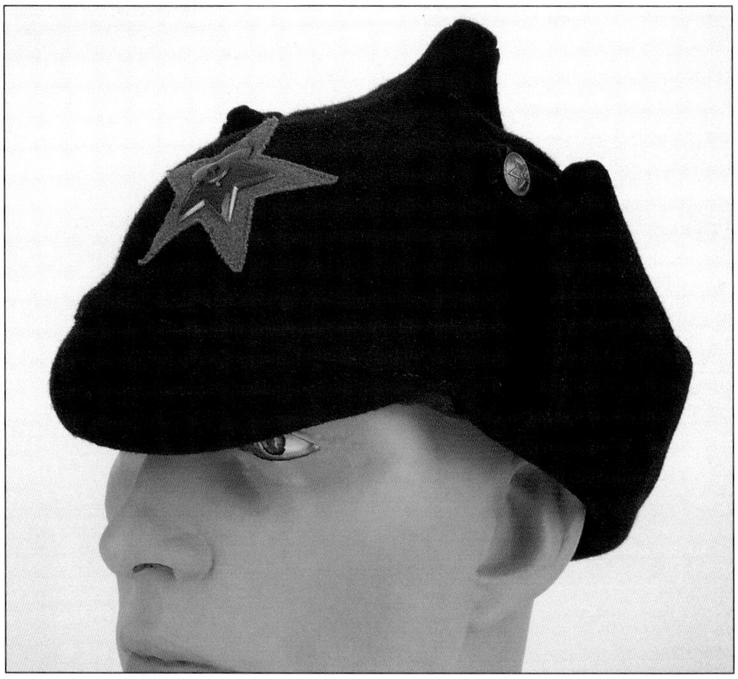

Above: Air Force Officer Budionovka in dark blue with light blue star. Right: Interior of Air Force Budionovka dated 1940.

Army Medical or Administration Budionovka. Both organizations used gray with a green star for branch colors.

Army Field Cap first introduced in 1924 worn by all branches.

Army Cavalry Officers visor cap with 1935 pattern two piece star.

Air Force Officer service dress visor cap with dark blue top in use until 1943.

Air Force visor cap made before the introduction of colored piping for Air Force in 1935.

Left: Navy enlisted mans cap. Made before1936 without the white piping.

A Naval Officer visor cap without piping is pre-1936.

Above: Air Force Senior Commander with 1935 pattern colored piping and a dark blue top and band. Right: Interior of Air Force Senior Commander visor cap.

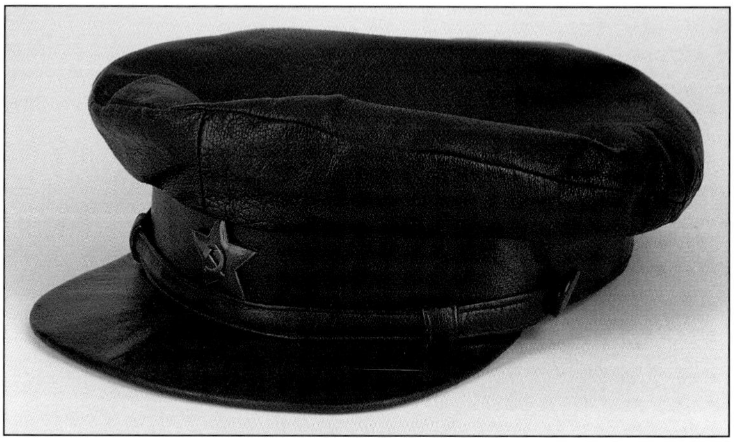

The leather visor cap intended for Armor Troops was also popular with the NKVD.

Armor Officers 1935 visor cap was regulation until 1943. Artillery and Armor troops both adopted the cap with an olive brown top. The gray top cap was worn by many officers in the field until the end of the war.

Field Cap for all branches of the Army with the 1935 officers pattern star.

Right: Artillery Officers cap with red piping and a black wool band.

White summer dress visor cap worn by Military and Political personnel. Regulations in 1940 introduced colored cap bands for the white top caps.

Senior Commander of Infantry wears raspberry piping and band. Marshal of the Soviet Union would be Red band and piping.

Staff College cadet visor cap.

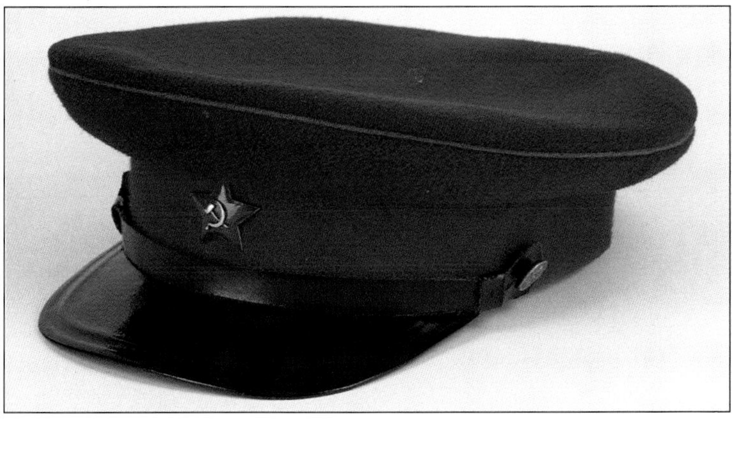

Cossack visor cap of Don Group.

Wine red band and white piping is the distinction for a Senior Commander of Staff College.

Senior Commander of NKVD, Internal Security. Gray top with brick red band and piping.

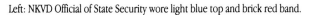

Left: NKVD Official of State Security wore light blue top and brick red band.

NKVD Official of Frontier Troops or Border Guards wore an emerald green top with dark blue band and red piping.

NKVD Officers summer dress.

Infantry visor cap with cotton top for summer use.

NKVD State Security enlisted grade visor cap. Note the one piece M-35 star.

Artillery summer visor cap made with multi-colored weave fabric.

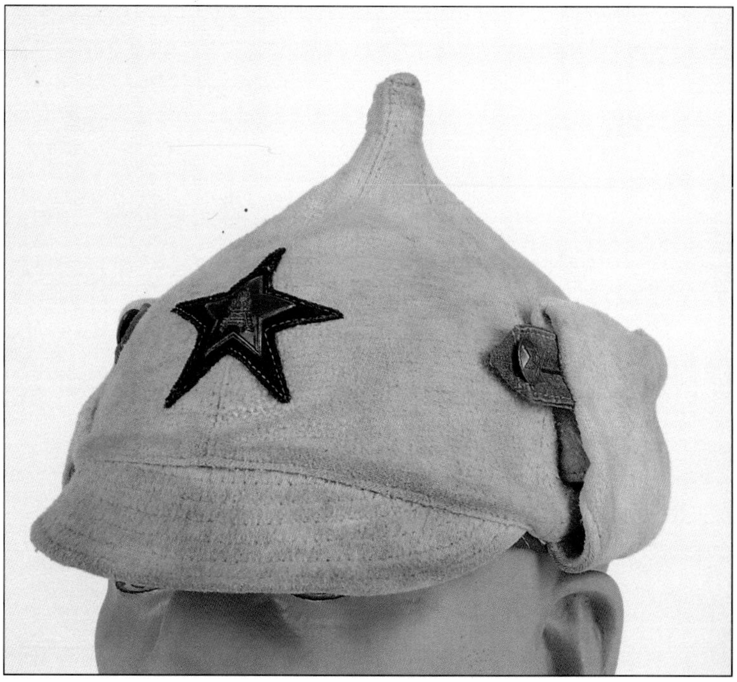

Budionovka for Train personnel. This cap is white cotton with a train on the enamel star rather than the hammer and sickle.

Enlisted grade Train Troops visor cap with red top and black wool or velvet band.

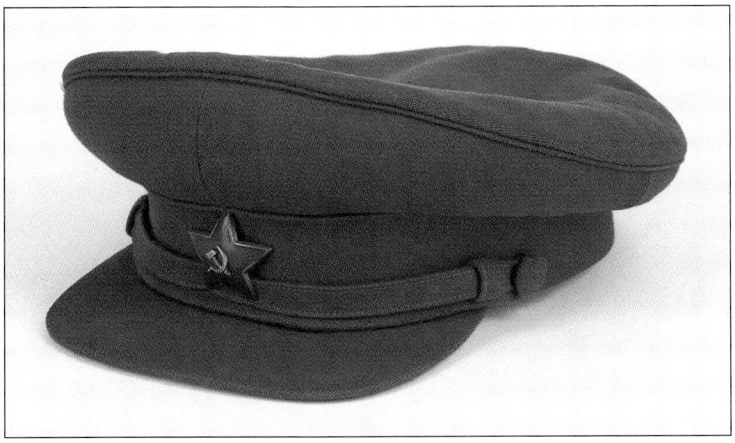

Army Field cap with Senior Commander star. After 1940 the large stars were often worn by officers of all ranks.

NKVD Commanders cap circa 1933. The exterior shape and visor design indicate the period of manufacture.

Right: Air Force field cap. The blue field caps were introduced in the mid 1920s and were in use as long as the blue uniform was in service.

Transportation Officers cap with light blue piping and black velvet band.

Army visor cap for Medical and Administrative personnel. The colors are green band and red piping.

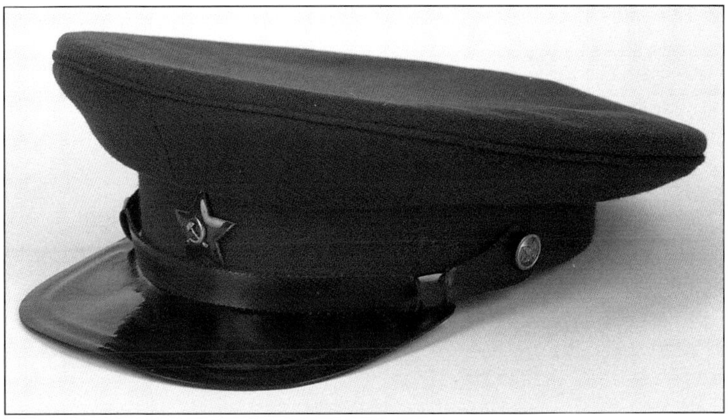

Transportation Official of the NKVD.

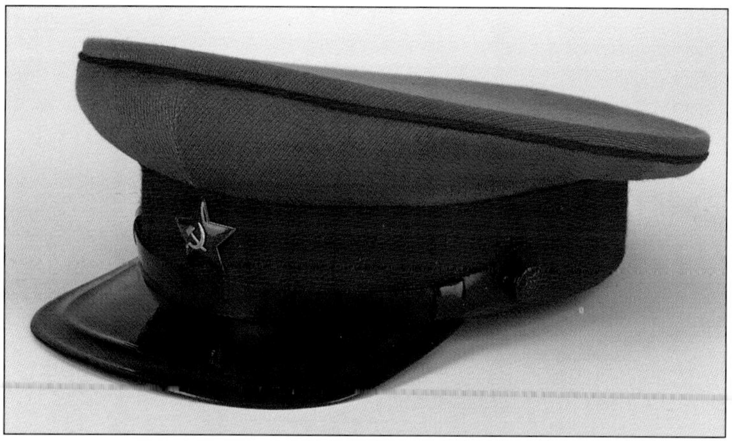

Army Infantry Officer. The lighter color cotton material was intended for summer use.

Army Visor cap for summer white dress. The Army used the white covers without piping.

Air Force Officer service and field cap. A wide variety of insignia was used within the wreath.

Armor Troops visor cap with steel gray top was regulation from 1935 through 1942. This example has a single ridge in the visor rather than the usual two.

Armor Troops Senior Commander. This example illustrates the "salt and pepper" fabric that was popular during the 1930s. Note the size of the Senior Commander star.

Air Force Officer service cap. Worn with the blue uniform until it was phased out in 1942.

Winter cap for Officer, Model 1940. Genuine lambs wool varieties were popular with officers.

Officer winter cap, 1940. This example is constructed of brown leather and lambs wool.

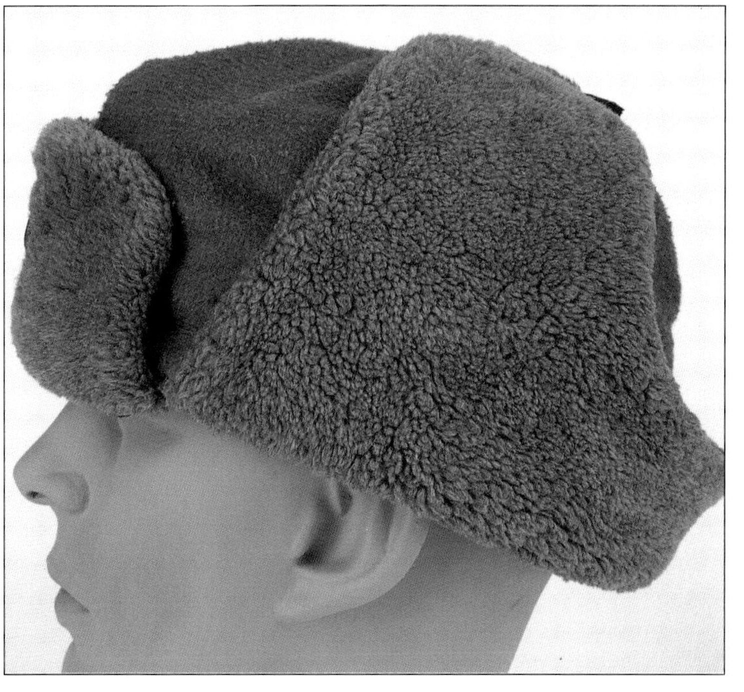

Left: Soldiers example of Model 1940 pile cap. The fur is a synthetic produced from cotton. The Russian name for it is "fish fur." Right: The ear flaps tie at the top when not in use. The front flap could be used as a visor.

General Officers cap. Crimson red band is used by Infantry Generals and Marshals. The round cap device for Generals was introduced in 1940.

Armor Officers visor cap. Steel gray with black band and red piping were the branch colors of Armor uniforms from 1935 to 1943. This example shows German influence with pink piping and the shortness and angle of the visor.

Right: Inside view of Armor Officers visor cap that has the "PKKA" marking and 1940 date.

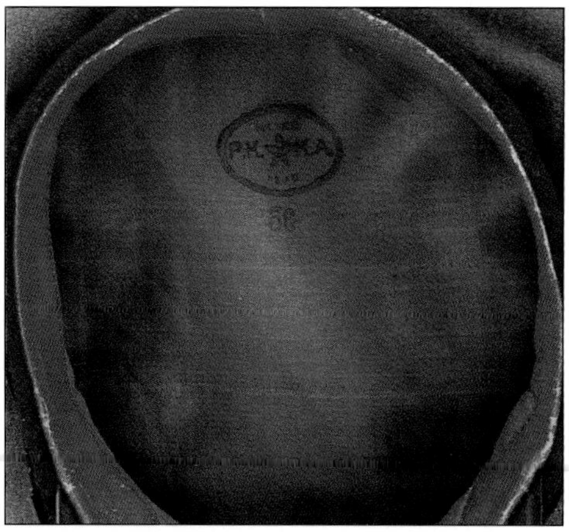

Artillery enlisted mans cap.

Visor cap NKVD General of Military Security.

NKVD enlisted man Military Intelligence.

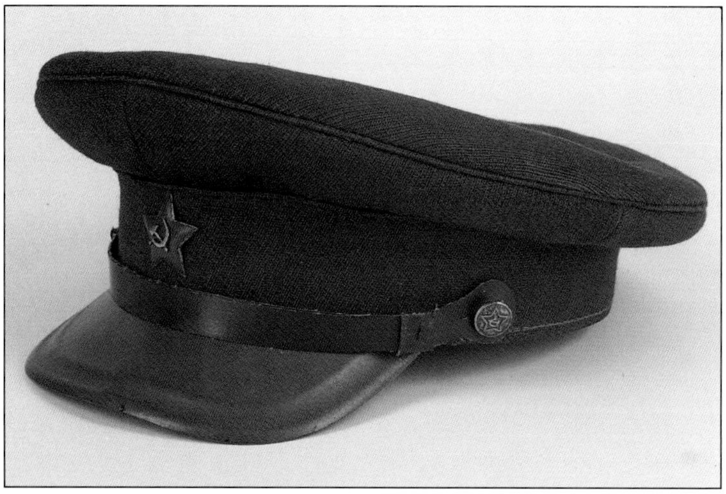

Field cap for Officer dated 1940. Olive drab visors and chin straps were produced in limited numbers from the late 1920s until the early 1940s. The cloth visor and chin strap were more common.

Army General cap, field dress. In 1940 regulation indicated that the black chin strap was to be worn with field dress. The gold double cord chin strap was to be reserved for service and dress occasions, however the gold chin strap was worn almost exclusively.

Infantry Officers visor cap.

Air Force Officer field dress visor cap. In addition to the red star, a metallic bullion wreath with upper wing and star insignia was introduced in the late 1930s. This combination of insignia remained in use throughout World War II. This early pattern working cap didn't have the sky blue band.

Army fatigue hat with Infantry color star. This cap was worn in tropical conditions and the border conflicts with Japan.

Naval Officers cap 1935 pattern.

Militia visor cap introduced in 1938. Militia duties were similar to usual police duties.

Infantry enlisted mans cap with 1935 pattern cap star.

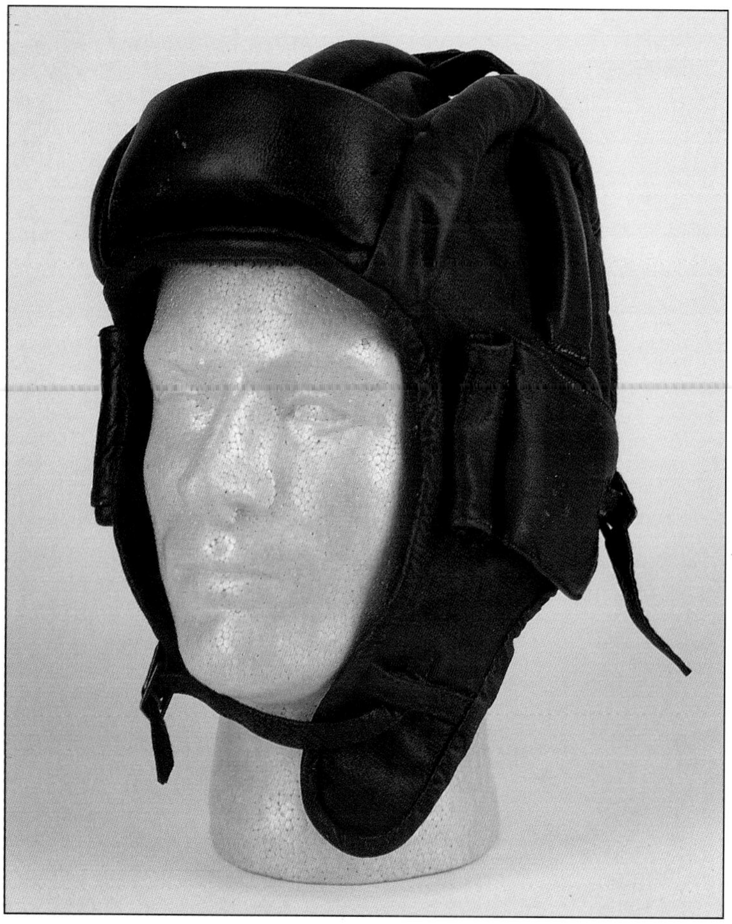

Left: Tanker Helmet. A pre-war leather example. Right: Side view of leather Tanker Helmet.

Cossack Officers cap. This Kubanka was worn by the Terek Cossacks.

Cossack Officers cap. The red top denotes the Kuban Cossack ethnic group.

General Officers cap 1940 parade dress. This pattern cap was worn with Artillery General Officers parade uniform. The service dress cap for Armor personnel would be the same as the parade dress, since their service color was also the parade color for all branches.

Artillery Officers cap manufactured in 1940. During 1939 and 1940 German styles influenced some Soviet uniforms. The shape and angle of this visor show German influence.

Army General Officers field cap with no branch color. This pattern cap became more common as the war progressed.

Artillery Officers cap. Dated 1940.

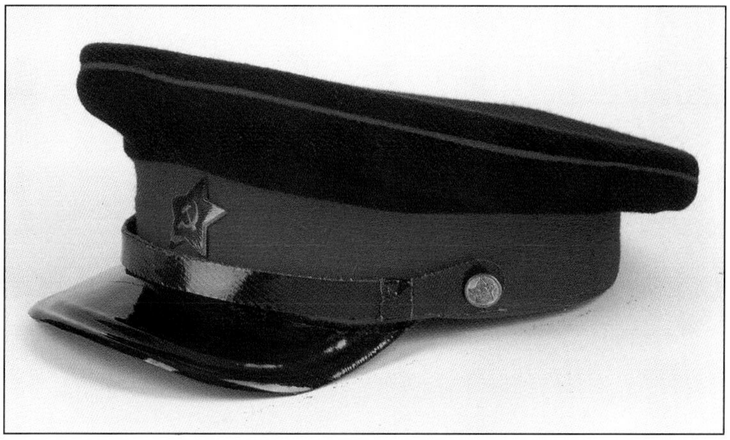

Military Cadet of Artillery School, circa 1943.

Generals field cap, circa 1942. The side buttons have eleven Republic banners and are painted green.

Naval dress and service cap for enlisted men.

Infantry visor cap. This cap has a round visor made in 1941. Period photographs show both styles of visor were worn at the same time.

Medical Officers cap 1942 showing wartime shortages. The top is rough reworked wool with a short visor to conserve material. The cap star is now a single piece for all ranks.

Technical Troops cap. The colors, dark blue piping and black band, were instituted in December 1935.

Cloth Field cap worn by officers throughout the war.

Cloth Field cap variation with gilt side buttons.

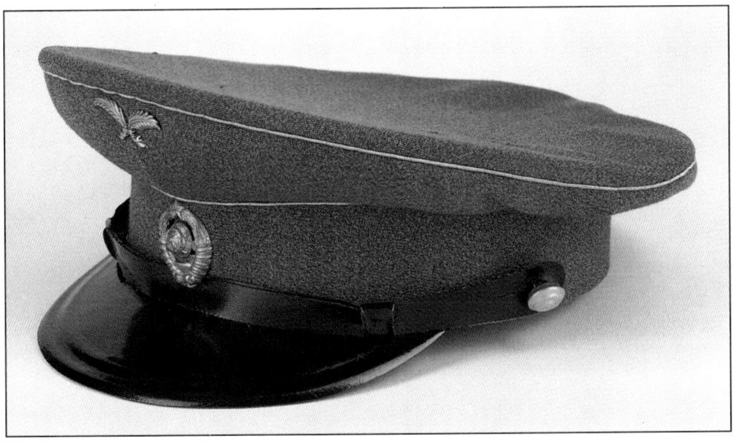

Diplomatic Corps visor cap. This was made in both gray and blue for full dress. The upper insignia are crossed quills and insignia on the band is the seal of the Soviet Union with eleven Republics.

Senior Militia Official. The badge and the side buttons represent the eleven Republics.

NKVD visor cap for enlisted ranks.

General of Artillery or Armor visor cap. By 1943 Armor Troops had adopted the standard Army colors.

General of Infantry visor cap. This gray cap was worn with the gray walking out dress tunic. Dark blue trousers or breeches with General's red stripes would complete the uniform.

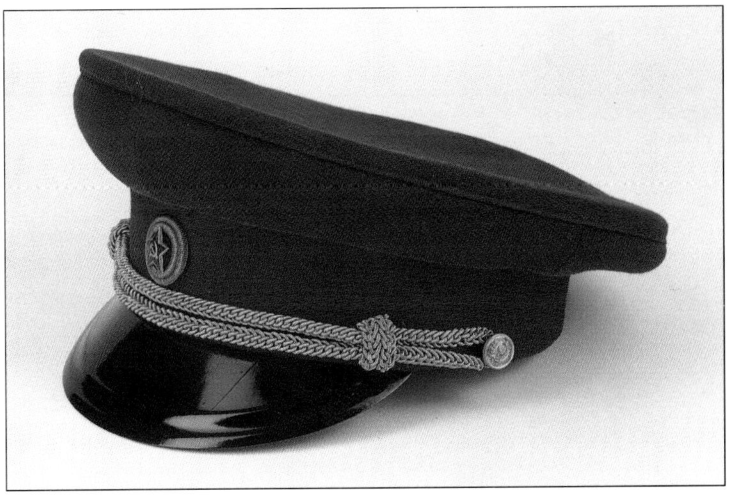

General of Infantry visor cap variation with round visor and two-piece insignia.

Air Force General visor cap. The cocard is light blue enamel behind the red star. General rank of other organizations also used their specific colors on the cocard. Known examples are: NKVD Frontier Troops-green, NKVD Military branch-dark blue, Army and NKVD State Security-red.

Air Force NCO and enlisted grades visor cap.

Naval Officer of Technical branch visor cap.

Air Force Officer with final pattern enamel insignia.

Naval Officer of the line visor cap.

Chemical Troops visor cap instituted in 1935. The band and piping are black.

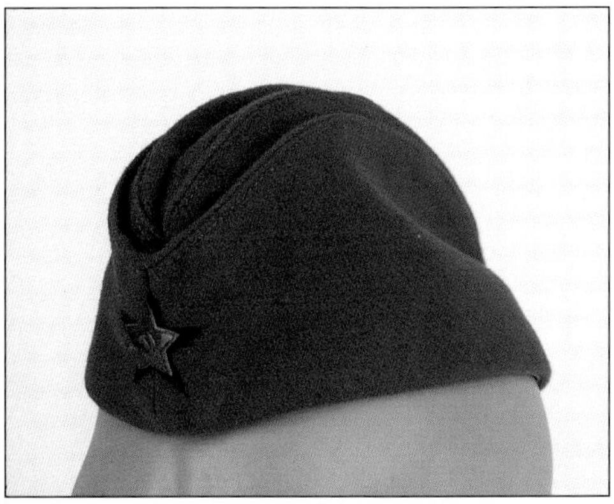

Left: Armor Troops Officer Pilotka or Overseas cap dated 1939. Colored piping for the respective branches was introduced in 1935. Enlisted personnel didn't have distinctive piping. Steel gray was obsolete by 1943, but the visor caps and pilotka's were used through the end of the war. Center: Infantry pilotka with raspberry piping. For a time NCOs were permitted to wear branch color piping without the cloth star. Right: Artillery pilotka with red piping.

Left: Chemical branch pilotka with star and black piping. Center: Transportation Officer pilotka with black star and blue piping. Right: Army summer enlisted pilotka dated 1938.

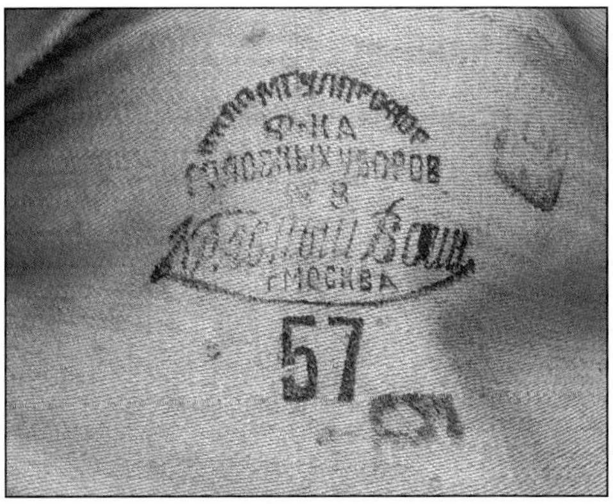

Left: Army enlisted pilotka variation with a stitched outline of the red star on the cap. Center: Inside view of Army enlisted grade pilotka. Right: Navy Petty Officer Pilotka.

Left: Army pilotka or overseas cap. Near the end of 1941 new regulations eliminated the piped overseas caps. The same unpiped Pilotka was to be worn by both officers and men. The existing piped caps were worn until replacements were needed. Center: Army Pilotka dated 1943. During 1941 and 1942 regulations ordered subdued insignia to replace the red enamel insignia. Cap stars and collar patch rank devices were now in field color. Not enough subdued insignia were issued and photographic evidence indicates that some commanders, especially in front line positions, ordered removal of the red enamel star from pilotka. Right above: Inside view of dated Army pilotka. Right below: Inside view of 1943 dated pilotka.

Profile of the 1936 helmet.

In the field, summer 1944.

Private, circa 1941, with cap star from early 1930s period visor cap.

Air Force officers with 1938 Pattern visor caps.

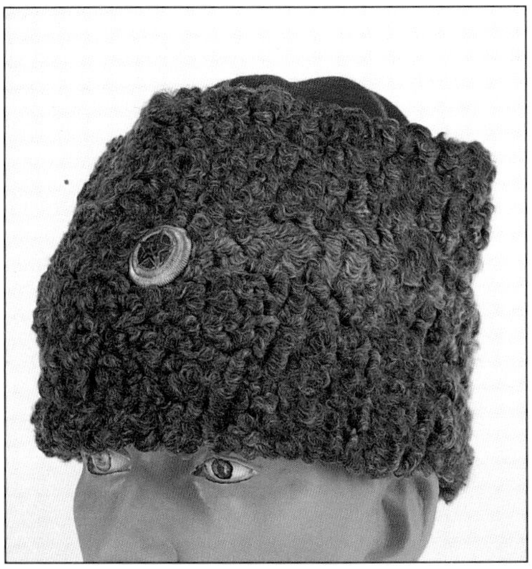

Army Generals Astrakan cap introduced in 1940. This cap has a red top with gold tape from side to side.

NKVD General Officer Astrakan cap with a dark blue top and dark blue enamel cap badge.

Army Colonel Astrakan cap. The top is gray with thin gold tape in the same pattern as a General. This version has flaps that can be folded down.

Infantry Officers pilotka with raspberry piping and red star.

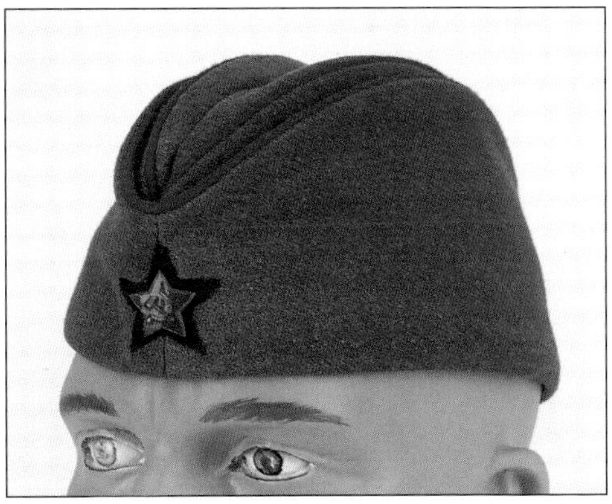

Artillery Officer pilotka with red piping and black star.

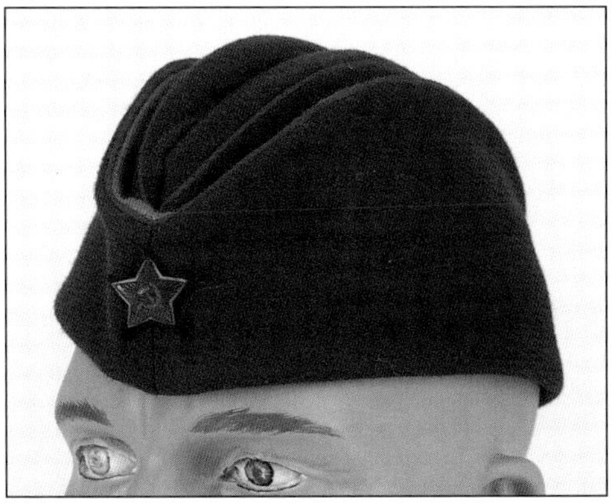

Manufacturing variation of Artillery Officer pilotka.

Air Force Officer pilotka. Photographic evidence indicates that the dark blue pilotka was worn with the dark blue service uniform as well as the field uniform.

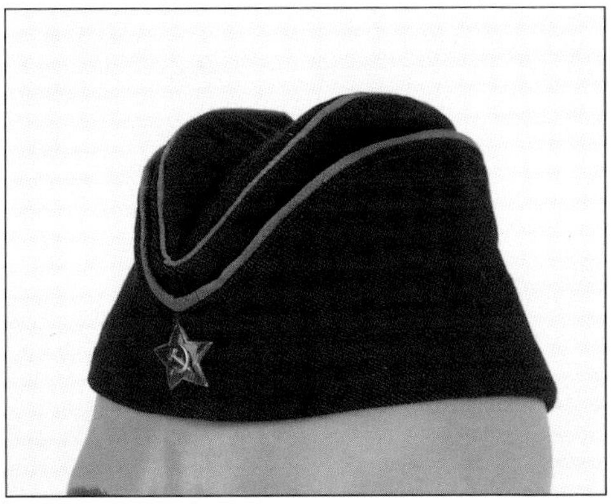

Air Force NCO pilotka. This cap was worn by a female sergeant of Engineering.

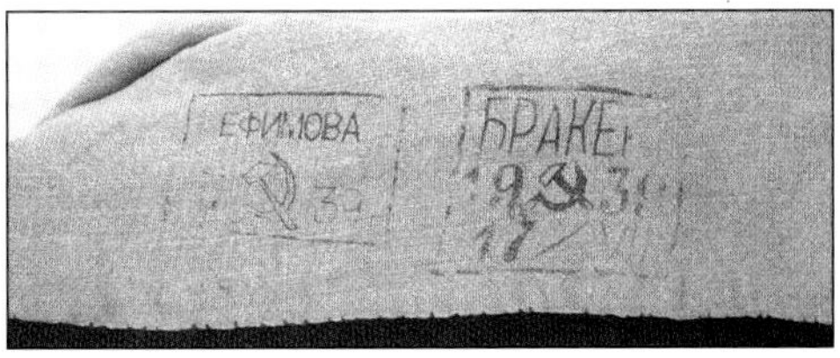

Inside view of Air Force pilotka.

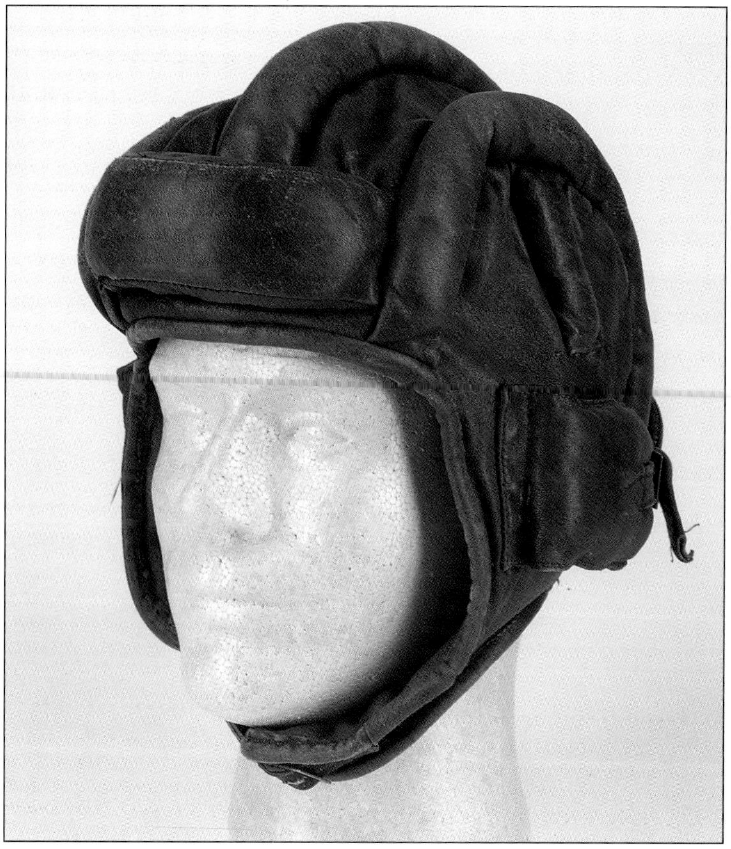

Pre-war leather tanker helmet.

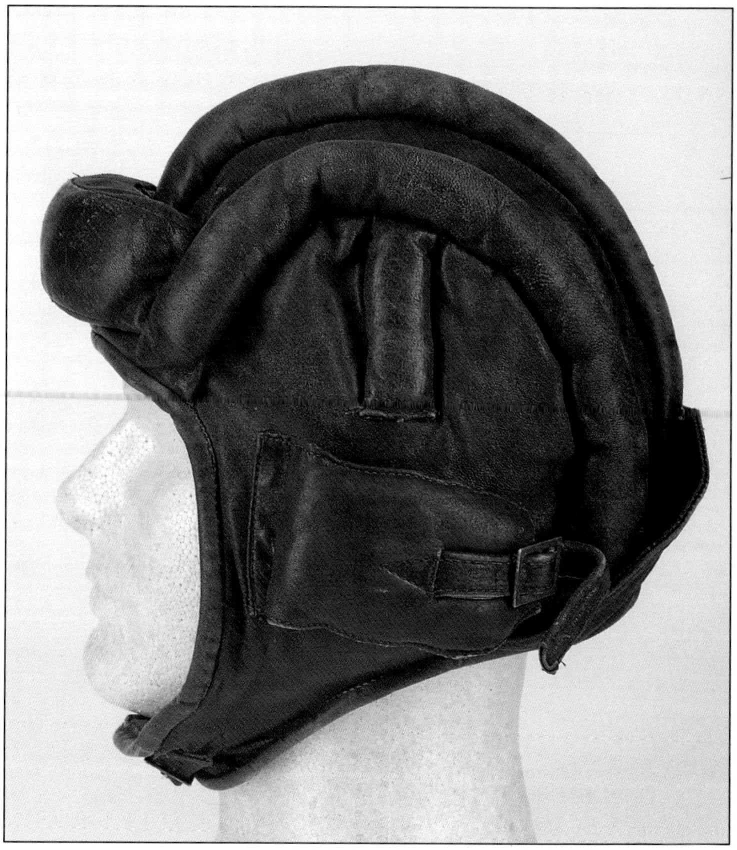

Side view of leather tanker helmet.

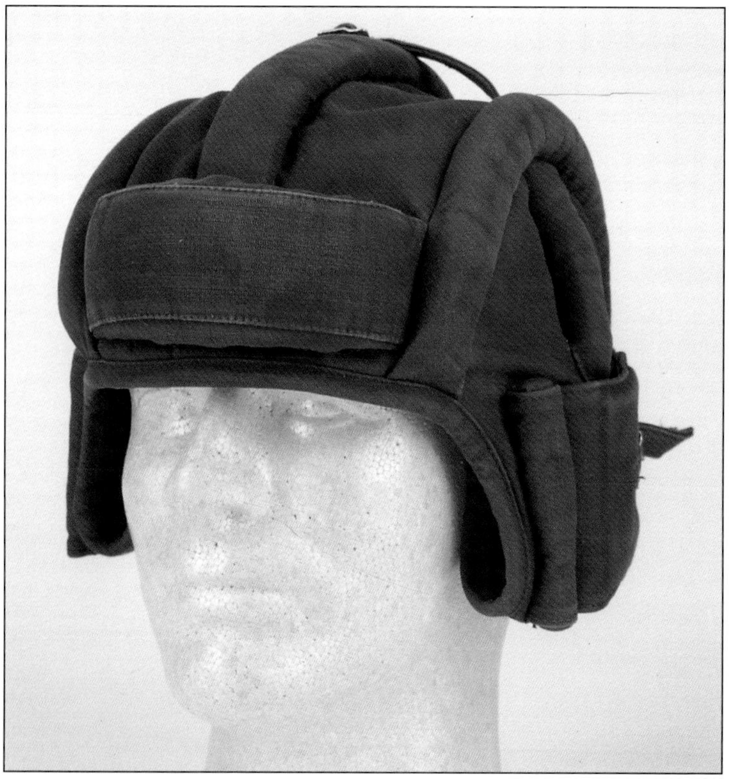

Wartime manufacture tanker helmet made of black canvas.

Side view of canvas tanker helmet.

Tanker helmet OD canvas.

Side view of OD canvas tanker helmet.

Right: Back flap showing 1943 date.

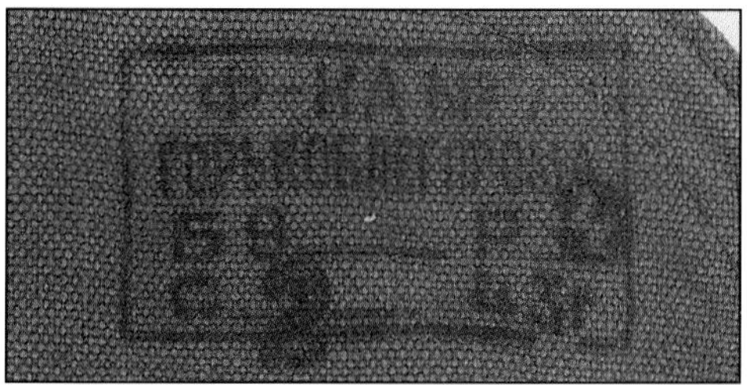

Army General Officer visor cap. An experimental model with olive brown top and red band with parade style embroidery worn with the Model 1943 service tunic.

Army General Officer visor cap for summer use. The silver chin strap indicates a technical branch such as Medical or Legal.

Naval Admiral visor cap. The gold insignia indicates a sea going officer.

Naval Admiral visor cap with silver insignia indicating Technical or Aviation branch.

Naval Captain and Commander visor cap. The single row of leaves on the visor was for Senior Naval ranks and the gold indicates a sea going officer.

Army General summer dress visor cap. This top is not removable but many removable covers were worn over wool tops.

Army General visor cap with gray dress top.

Marshal of the Soviet Union parade dress visor cap. This pattern was in use from February 1943 until April 1945.

Army General visor cap parade dress,1943.

Air Force visor cap parade dress, 1943. The gray parade dress uniforms were replaced by the wave green for Generals in 1945.

Army General visor cap Model 1940. Use of the red band and piping was broadened to include Generals of the Infantry. The 1935 regulation had reserved red for Marshal of the Soviet Union.

Marshal of the Soviet Union victory parade dress visor cap adopted in 1945. The new parade dress uniform retained the 1943 pattern visor cap only changing the top color to wave green.

NKVD parade dress visor cap for Generals, Model 1943.

Army General visor cap. Both the Administration and Medical branches used the green band, red piping and silver chin strap.

General of Engineers victory parade dress visor cap with burgundy piping and band.

General of Infantry victory parade dress visor cap with red band and piping.

General of Armor/Artillery victory parade dress visor cap with black band and red piping.

Air Force General parade dress, 1945. *(Photo by Les Kirby)*

General of Infantry victory parade dress visor cap with red band and piping.

Navy Admiral parade dress, 1945. *(Photo by Les Kirby)*

Right: Inside view of General Officer victory parade visor cap Model 1945.

Marshal of the Soviet Union victory parade. The multi-colored embroidery is a manufacturing variation.

General of Technical Branch victory parade visor cap. Technical branches are Legal, Medical and Administration.

Technical General victory parade visor cap with manufacturing variation.

CHAPTER SIX

Trousers and Breeches

A wide variety of trousers and breeches were worn by the Soviet Military from the revolution to the end of World War II. Branch of service and rank often can be identified by the color and style of trousers and stripes. The style and fabric choices were often dictated by end use of the trousers. Durable fabric with reinforced construction was necessary for field wear while more formal trousers were made of finer fabrics. Wartime shortages of strategic material also affected design and fabric. Study of period photographs and film footage gives the collector a good overview of trousers and breeches.

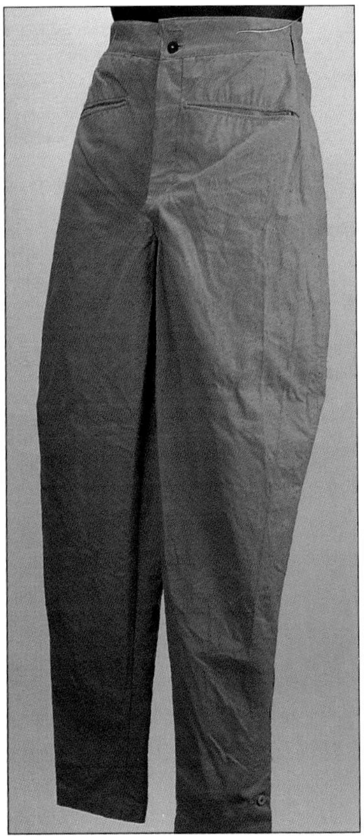

Rough cotton trousers for Army dating from the 1920s.

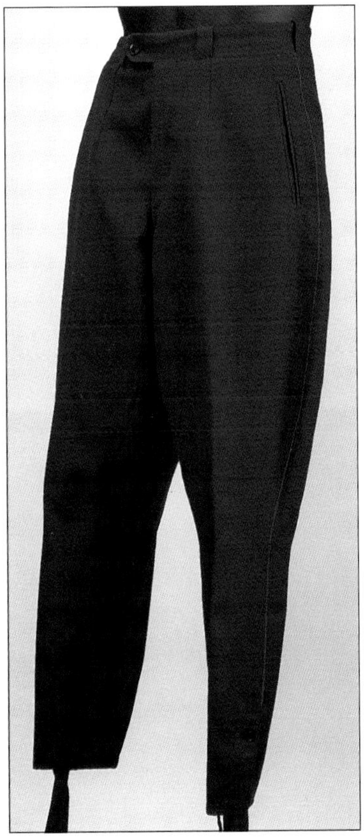

Officers pattern trousers with branch color piping on leg. This type of trouser was used through the end of the war.

Tank crew leather trousers. Internal markings indicate date of manufacture was 1937.

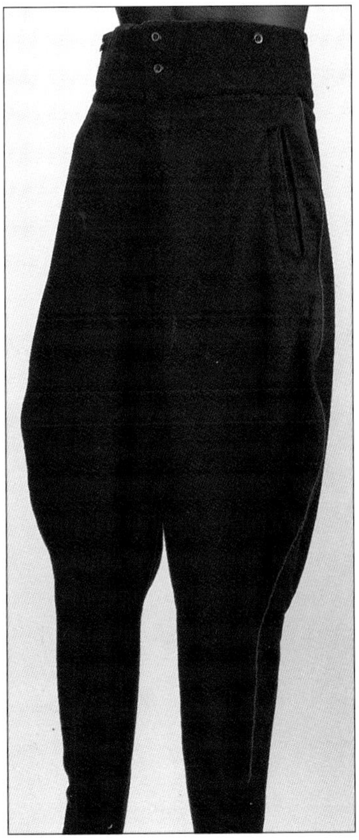

Officers pattern breeches in use from 1930.

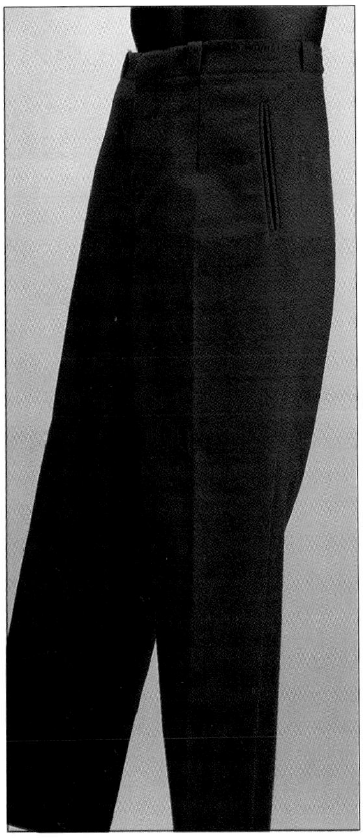

Steel gray Armor Officer trousers with red piping. These trousers were regulation from 1935 until 1943.

Infantry piped trousers in olive brown. This service and field color was often worn instead of the standard blue trousers.

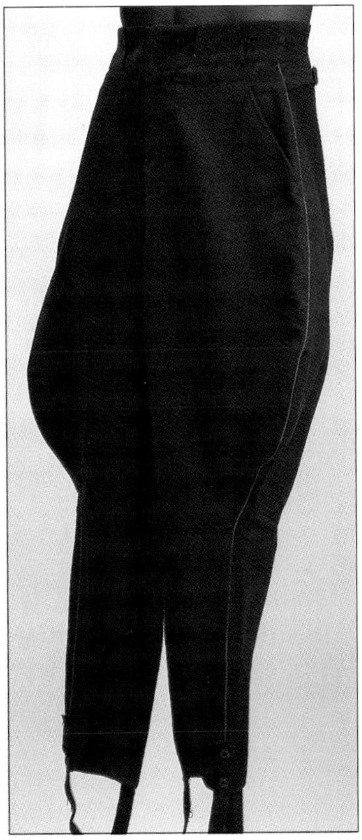

Air Force breeches for Officers. These were regulation from 1935 through the war.

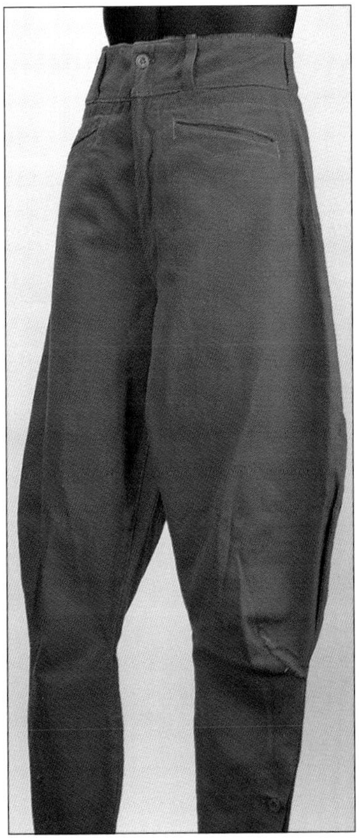

Cavalry breeches made of heavy cotton dated 1940.

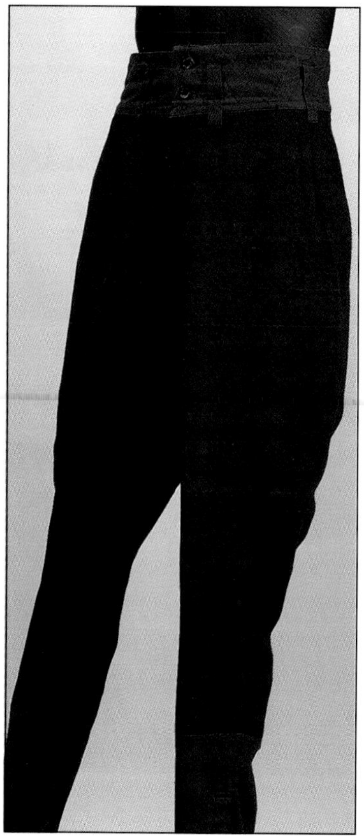

Army trousers without colored piping worn by sergeants after 1935.

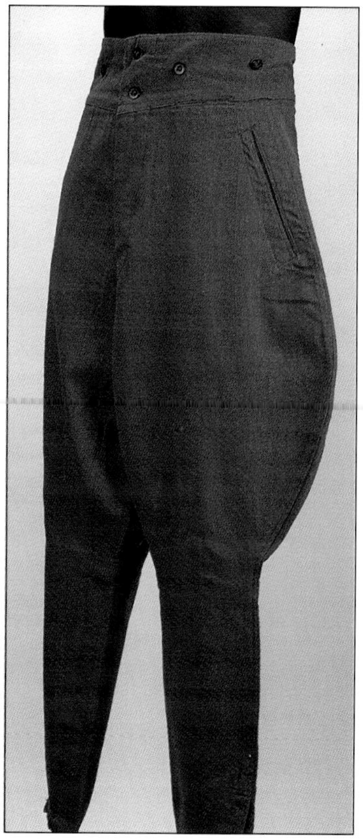

Trousers for soldiers from 1935 through the war.

Coveralls for Armor personnel. This example is from 1941.

Collar of coverall indicates Major Armor Troops.

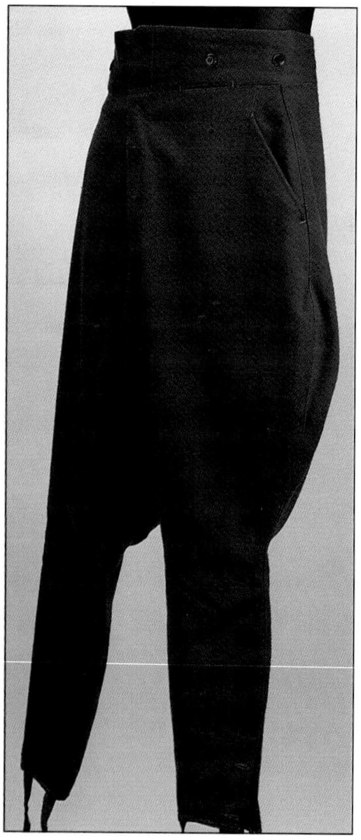

Breeches for Armor Officer instituted in 1935.

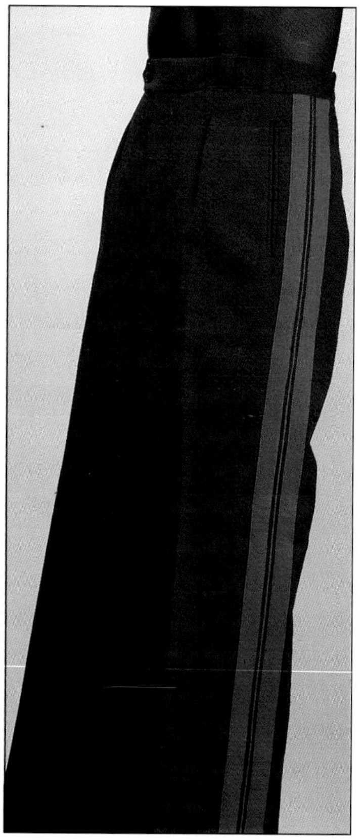

Trousers for Air Force General with double stripe introduced in 1940.

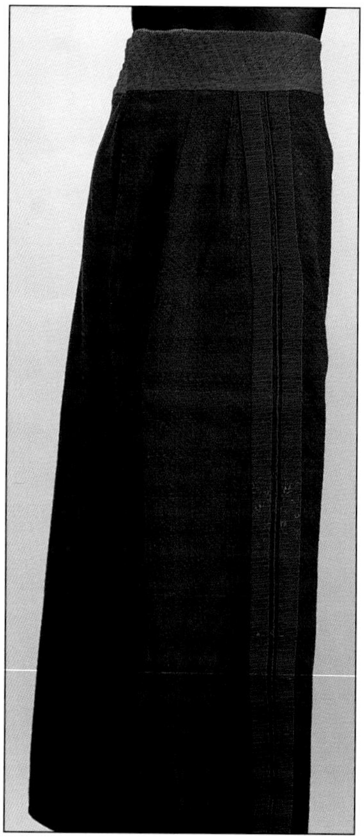

Breeches for Army General used as service and field dress.

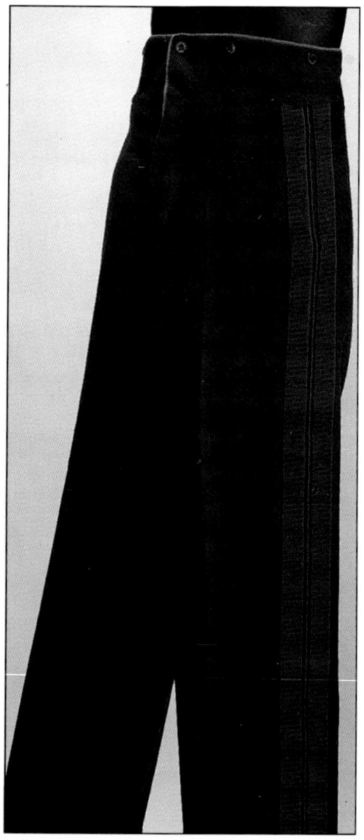

Another example of General trousers in blue.

CHAPTER SEVEN

Assorted Military and Personal Items

Nothing gives life to a collection of militaria like accoutrements. Items such as swords, daggers, badges, insignia and personal papers filling in gaps historically, as well as a wall or shelves for the collector. Many clues needed to date a cap or uniform can be found in small variations. A short lived change in the style and material of a cap or a tunic specific to a campaign, or a particular leader, can pinpoint dates for the collector.

Sleeve insignia of Regiment Commander, 1918 pattern.

Sleeve insignia of Bolshevik leader, Turkistan.

"Revolutionary Court Martial Tribunal" sleeve insignia instituted in 1922.

NKVD collar tabs from top to bottom: 1.) Transportation, 2.) Internal Security, 3.) Frontier Troops, 4.) State Security.

Collar tabs from top to bottom: 1.) Frontier Troops, Captain Field tabs, 2.) Armor Captain. 3.) Air Force Captain, 4.) Artillery Captain.

Cavalry shoulder tabs sewn together before issue.

Three variations of sleeve insignia worn by Political Commissar. At least one other color has been observed. The star is light blue with gold hammer and sickle.

Air Force sleeve insignia top to bottom: 1.) Pilot, 2.) Engineer, 3.) Balloon Pilot.

NKVD Official sleeve insignia for Political Education.

Marshal of Soviet Union parade and service dress 1943.

Left: Marshal of Soviet Union field dress. Center: Admiral of the Fleet, the highest rank of Naval personnel during World War II. Right: Artillery Major Technical parade and service dress.

Left: Air Force 1st Lieutenant field dress. Center: Infantry Lieutenant parade and service dress. Right: NKVD Private, Internal Security.

Left: Master Sergeant, Medical Corps. Center: Colonel Supply Corps parade and service dress. Right: The shoulder boards were usually attached using a loop on the shoulder and a buttonhole with tie through on the board.

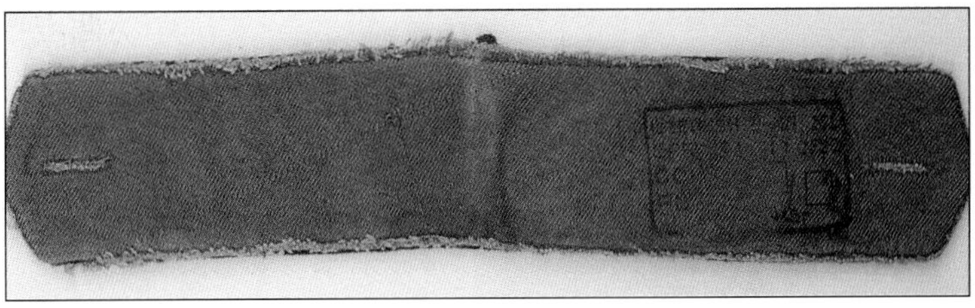

Left: Army Private shoulder straps. This example would be cut in half and the ends sewn into the shoulder seams of the tunic. Right: Markings on the underside of the one piece shoulder strap shows production date in 1945.

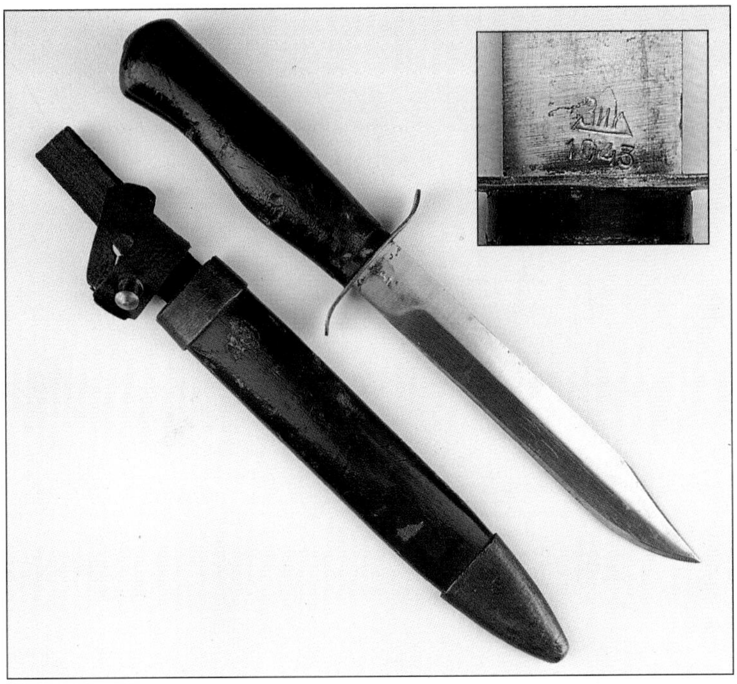

Soviet combat knife produced in 1943. The handle and scabbard of this knife are made of wood with black enamel finish.

Top: Petty Officer visor cap insignia. Bottom: Two patterns of Soviet Merchant service.

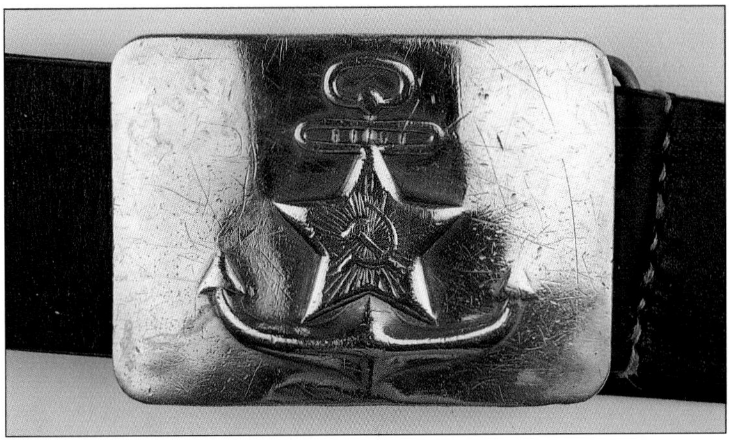

Naval enlisted mans belt introduced before the war.

Russian field art modification of a German belt buckle "into" a Russian buckle.

NKVD sleeve insignia worn on upper sleeve of each arm.

Left: The Star belt buckle for officers was introduced in 1935. It was issued for service and dress belt but was so popular that many officers wore it continuously, including field use. Right: Three enlisted pattern belts: the Sergeant Major belt with the same decorative design as an officers belt; the enlisted mans leather uniform belt; and leather and canvas belts that were introduced to conserve leather supplies.

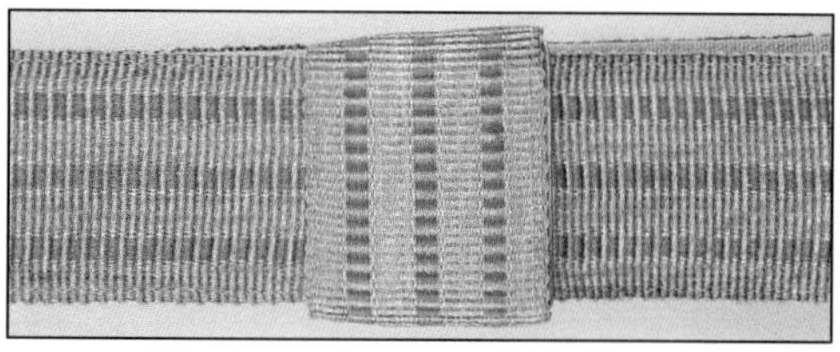

Above: Air Force General victory parade belt. Below: Detail of Air Force General victory parade belt.

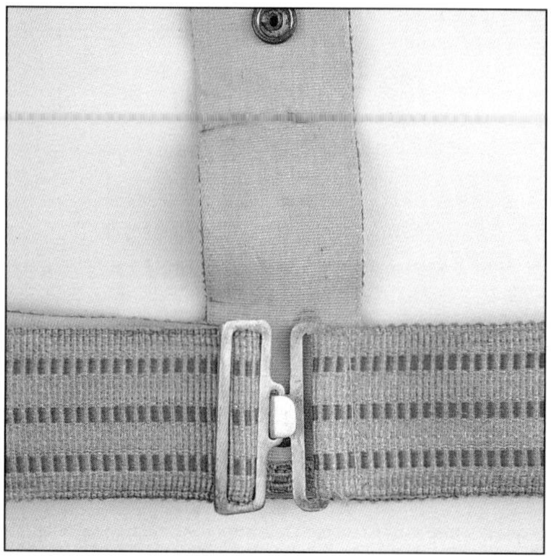

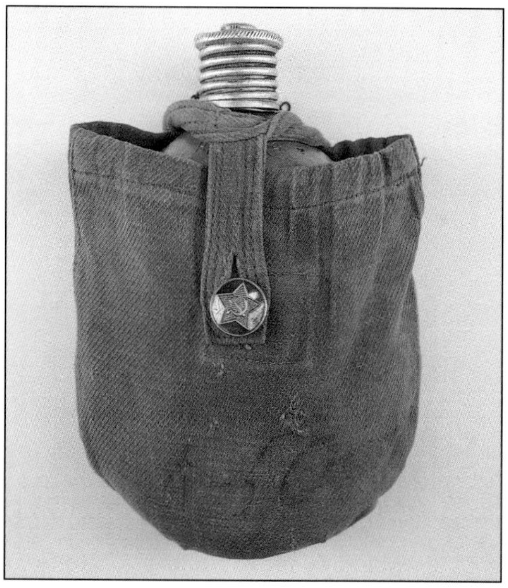

Above: The button on this canteen bears the mark of New York manufacturer indicating lend lease production. Below: A canteen bearing the Regiment and Company Designation, PKKA, "Peoples and Peasants Red Army."

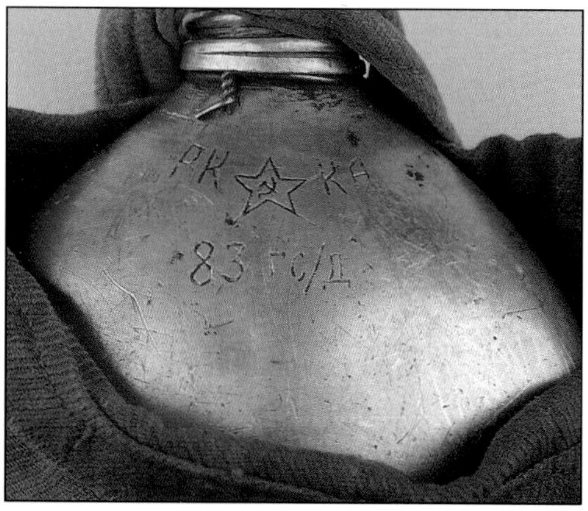

Field binoculars dated 1944.

Right: Model 1940 General Officers sword with chrome plated scabbard.
Far right: Top view of General Officers sword.

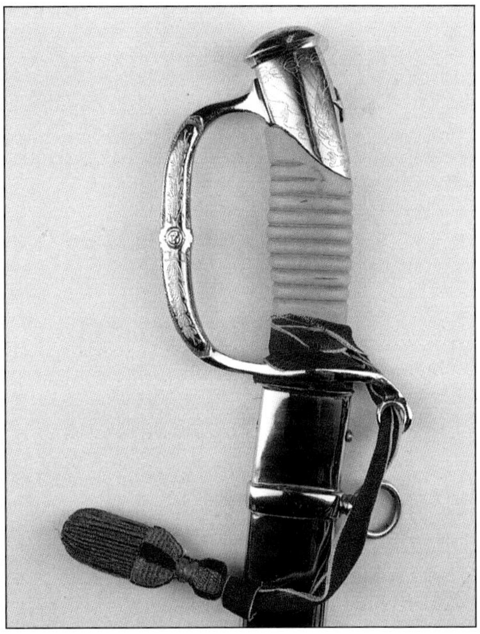

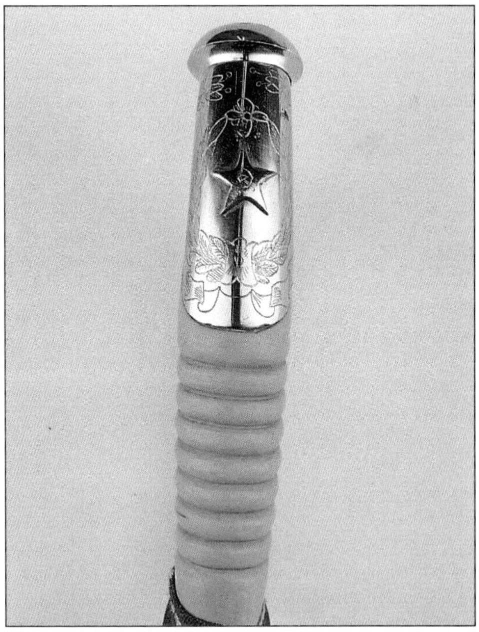

Right: Service and field pattern General Officers sword carried by many Generals and Marshals in the Victory Parade of June1945. The sword is post 1936 with the Eleven Republic seal.
Far right: Top view of Generals sword.

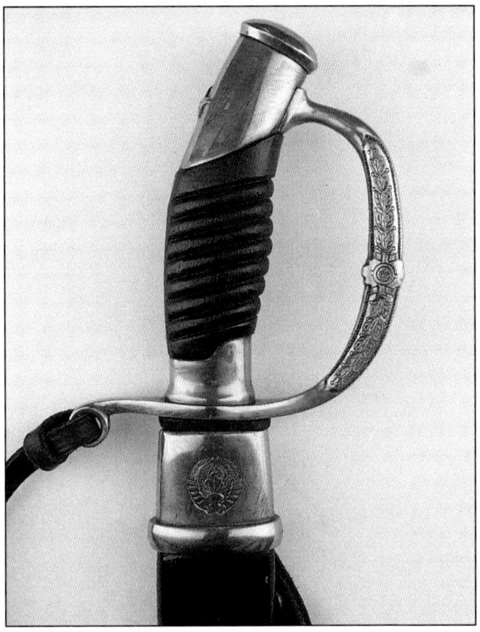

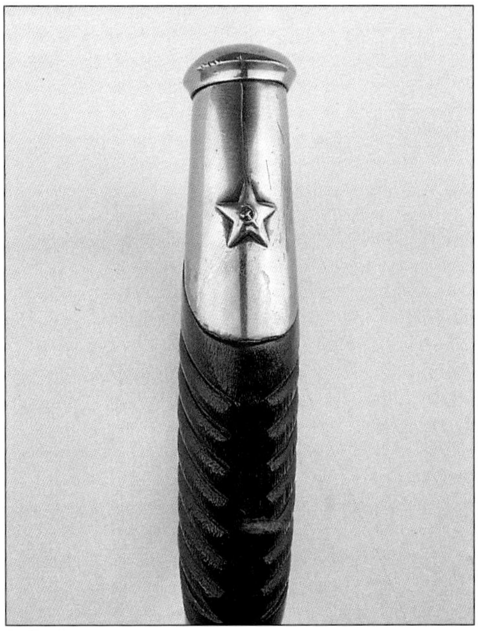

Right: Officers pattern Shasta or sword. This pattern was also referred to as a Cossack Saber. Officer pattern swords didn't have provisions for a bayonet.
Far right: Top view of Officers pattern sword.

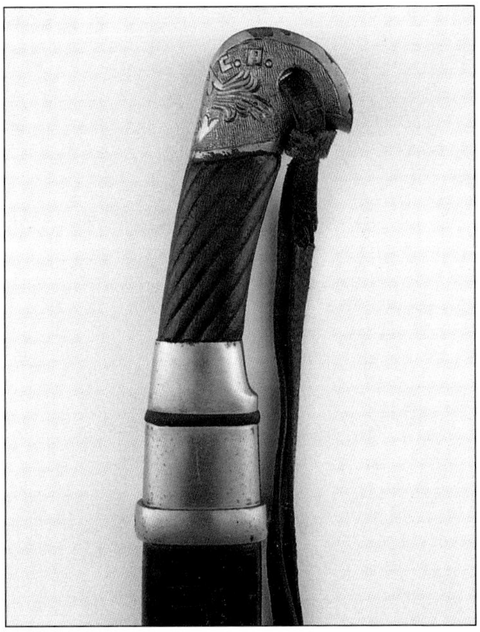

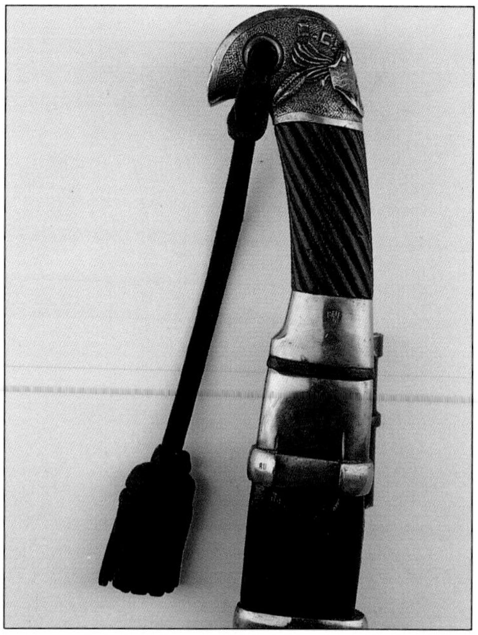

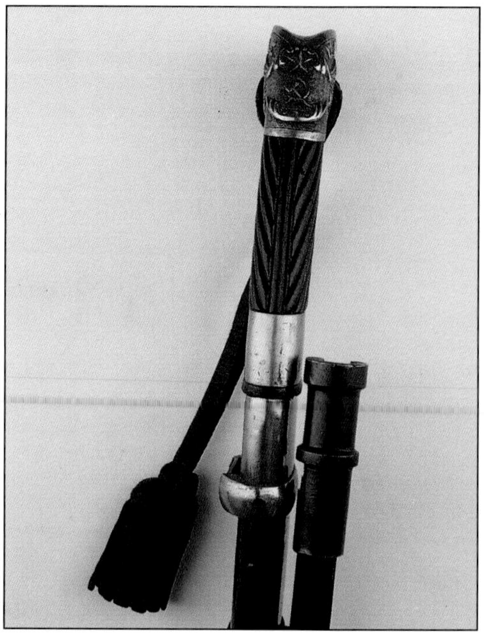

Above left: Enlisted mans pattern sword with bayonet provision. Center: The slot on the upper scabbard fitting will accept a leather harness. Right: Top view of common soldiers sword hilt.

Right: Cossack pattern Officers sword manufactured in 1942. A simplified star design on the pommel instead of the usual hand engraving was chosen because it required less manufacturing time. Far right: Top view of the 1942 Officers sword.

Below left: A 1942 production Cossack pattern enlisted mans sword made without the detailed decoration and fine finishing of earlier swords. The brass and steel components have a rough finish. Center: Date and arsenal marking. Right: Top view of Cossack pattern enlisted mans sword.

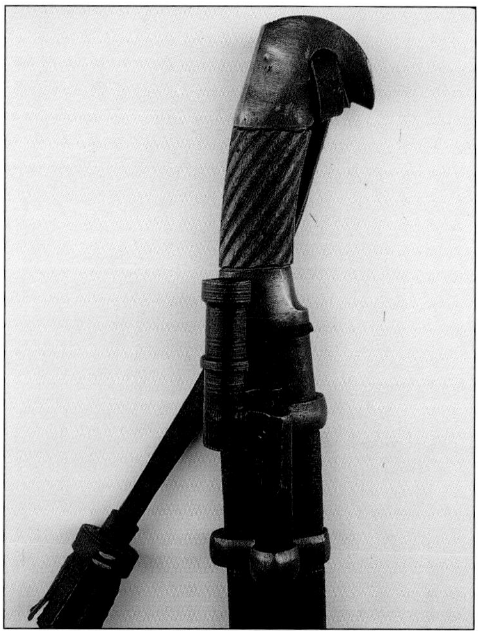

Right: This officers pattern sword made in 1945 shows that war production pressure had eased allowing more time and expense for the manufacture of non essential items. This sword incorporates the pre war hand engraving on the hilt as well as high quality finishing. Steel was used for the fittings since brass was still a strategic material.
Far right: Top view of 1945 Officers sword.

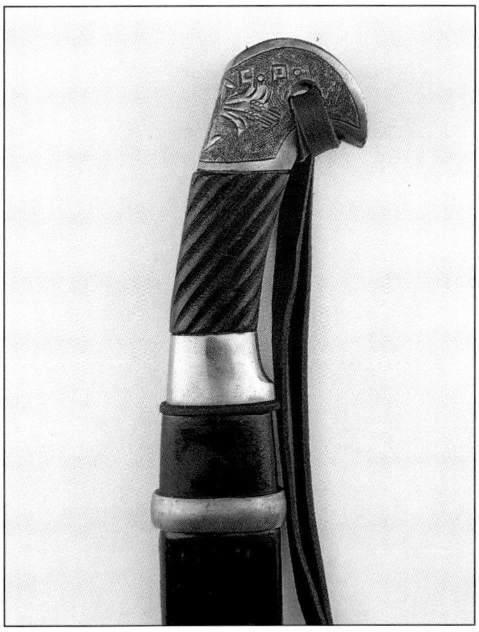

Right: Model 1940 General Officers dagger with all chrome fittings and blued steel scabbard. These daggers were worn for dress and parade.
Below: The chrome plated blade of General Officers dagger.

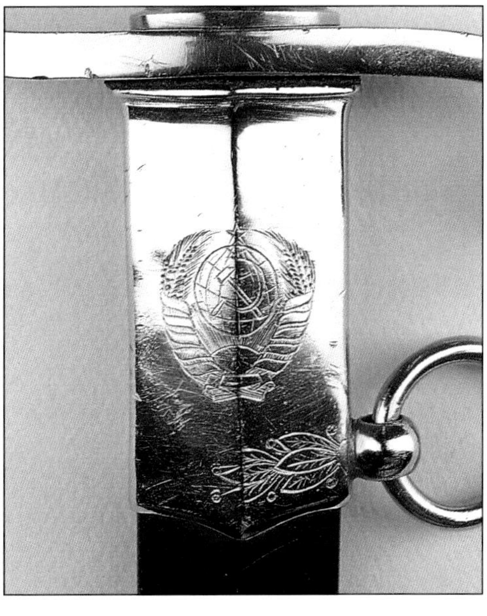

Left: Detail on dagger showing seal of Soviet Union with eleven Republics.
Far left: Pommel top of General Officers dagger.

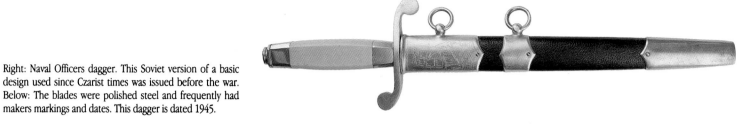

Right: Naval Officers dagger. This Soviet version of a basic design used since Czarist times was issued before the war. Below: The blades were polished steel and frequently had makers markings and dates. This dagger is dated 1945.

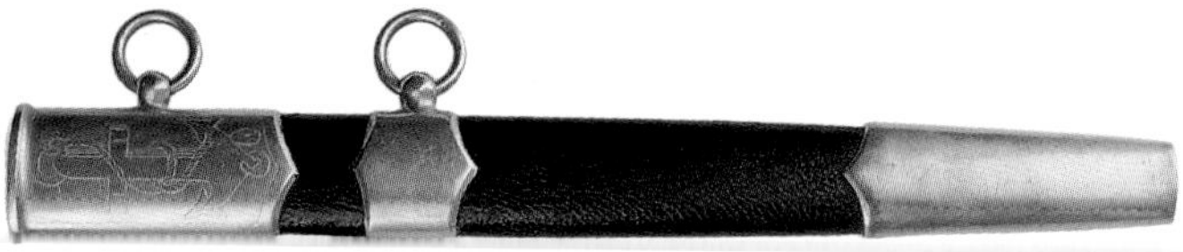

Below: Navy daggers attached to hangers.

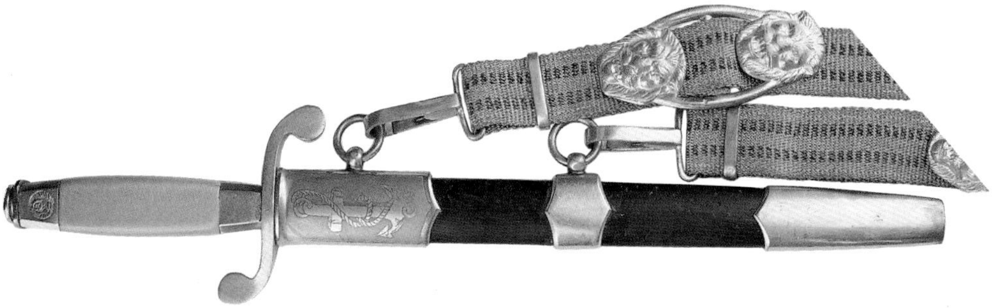

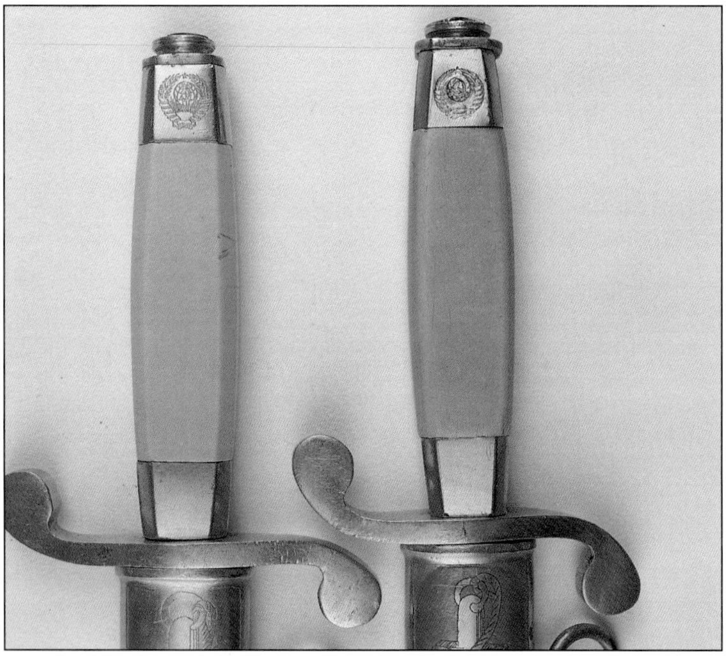

Two different dagger hilts. Note the eleven Republics seal.

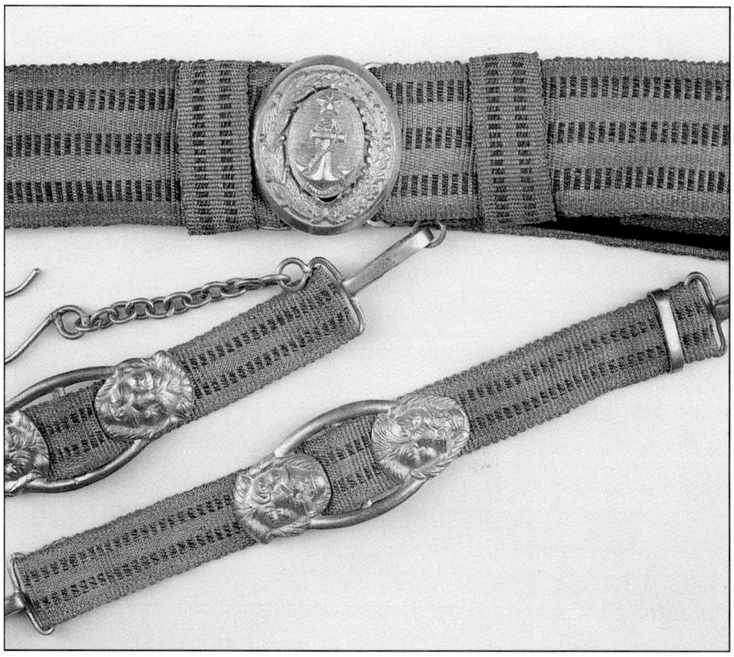

Dress belt with dagger hangers.

Left: Smoking was very popular. These photos show examples of the paraphernalia used at the time. Silver Smoking case with gold wash. Center: Decorations indicate this cigarette case was given to the foreman of a brewery in 1933. Right: Patriotic cigarette cases were usually given as a reward.

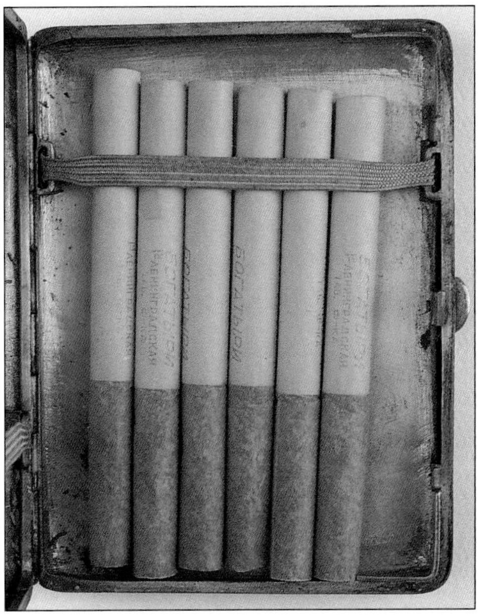

Left: This case was awarded to Border Guards for Proficiency. Center: The seal of the Soviet Socialist Republic of Armenia decorates this cigarette case. The bottom area of the inscription reads "Workers of the World Unite." Right: Interior of cigarette case complete with vintage Russian cigarettes.

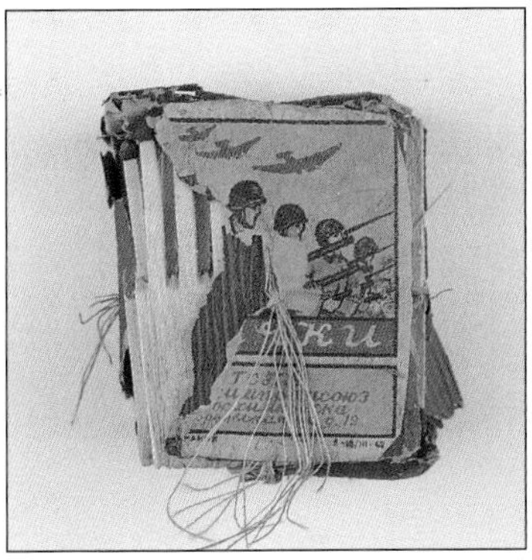

Above left: Wood matches from the war. Right: Opposite side of war time matches.

Right: Three war time cigarette lighters. Patriotic inscriptions such as "Death to Fascists Invaders" was a common slogan.

Left: Mounted Red Cavalryman with 1922 pattern uniform.

Lenin bust, circa 1940.

Lenin bust, cast iron, circa 1930.

Above: Gilded metal and enamel Stalin plaque, circa 1937.
Far left: Bronze plaque of Stalin in commemoration of the Eighteenth Party Congress.
Left: Bronze on wood Stalin plaque with facsimile signature of Stalin. This type of plaque would have been given as an award.

Patriotic statue of a soldier.

A popular style of Stalin bust. One is bone china and the other is bronze, post 1943.

Patriotic sculpture of soldier.

Cast bronze Stalin statue.

Patriotic statue of a Cossack.

Right: 1932 Nagent Revolver. A typical small arm used in World War II.

Right: Opposite side of the Nagent showing loading gate for cartridges.

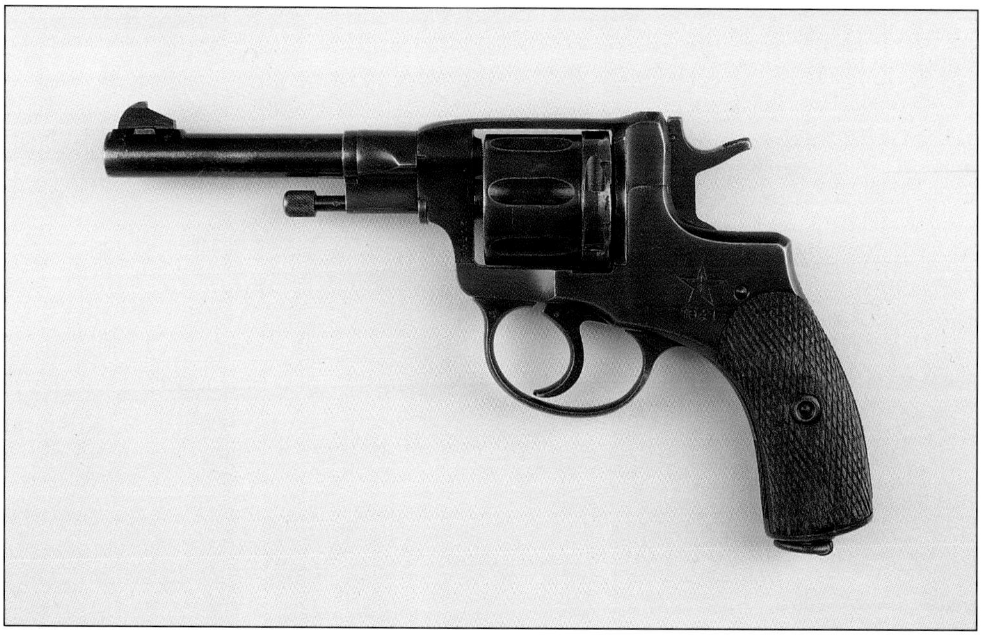

Right: 1941 Nagant Revolver. Although this weapon was outdated by more modern designs, it was produced and used through 1944.

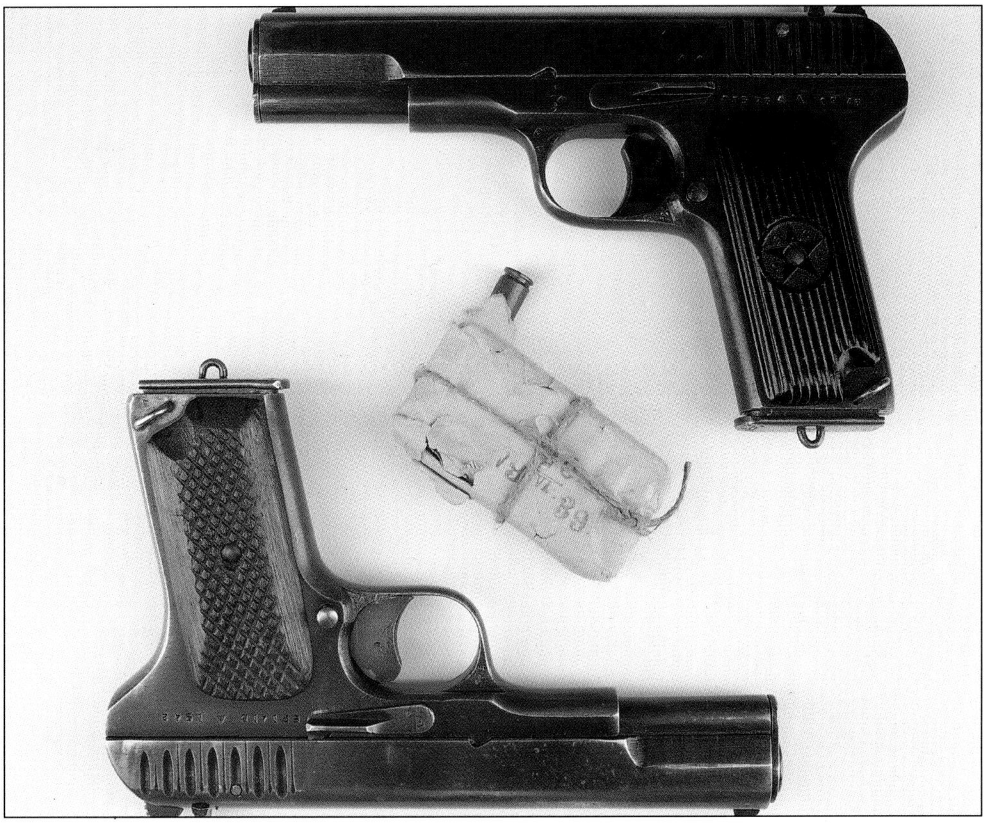

The TT33 Tokarev pistol was the standard pistol of the Soviets. The example with wood grips is a 1942 specimen.

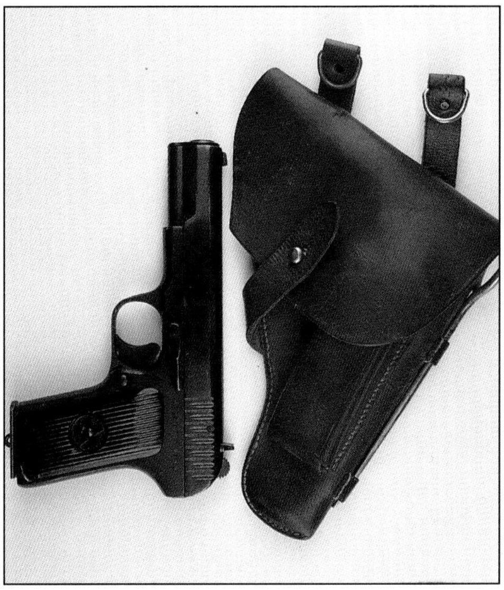

1944 production TT33 Tokarev pistol with holster. The grips are a bakealite material. A cleaning rod was often attached to the holster front. The D rings on the holster straps indicate that this pattern was intended to be used with the field belt kit.

TT33 Tokarev pistols viewed from other side.

1939 Tokarev TT33 pistol and holster front and rear views.

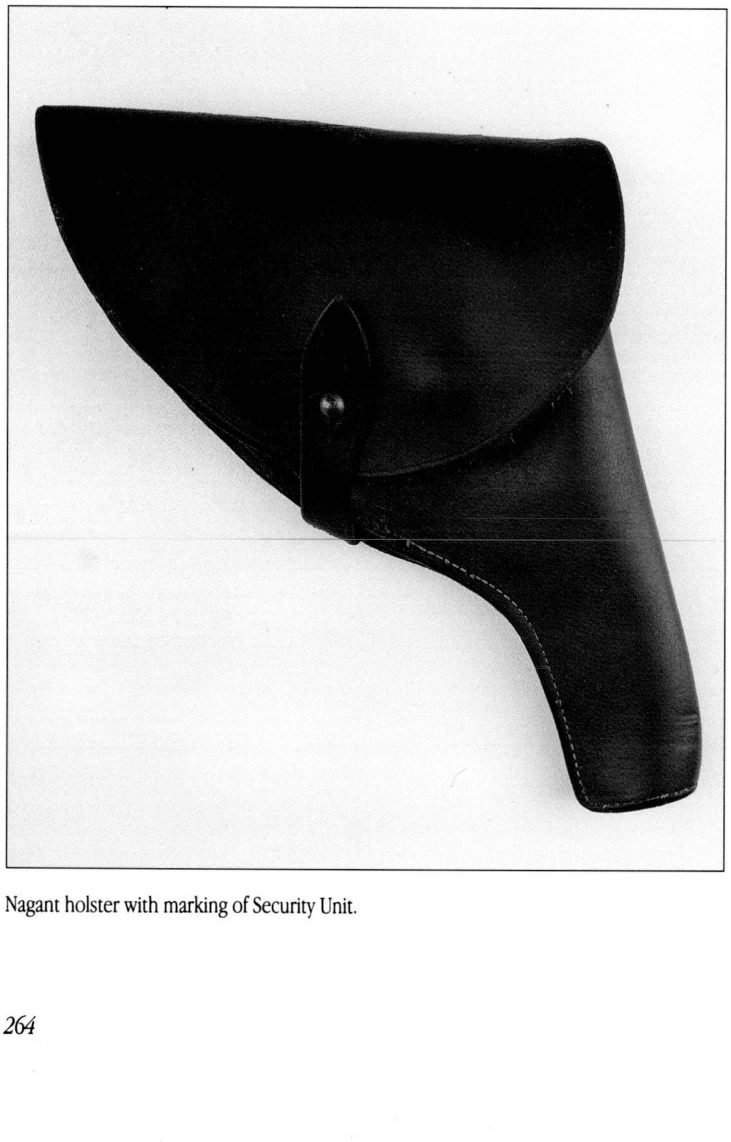

Nagant holster with marking of Security Unit.

Open Nagant holster.

1944 production Nagant revolver.

Opposite side of 1944 Nagant revolver.

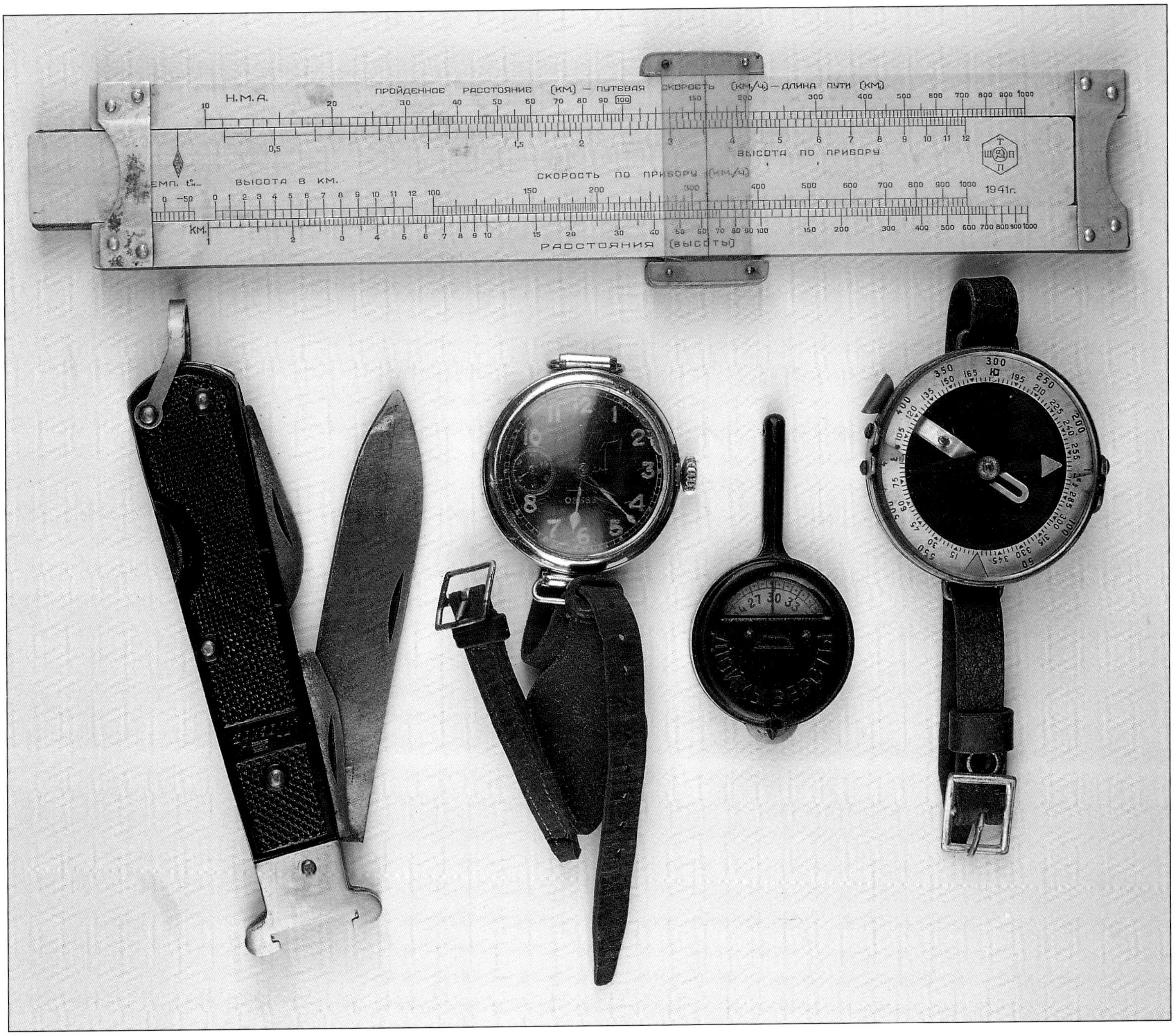

Miscellaneous items carried by Artillery Officer 1942-1943.

Model 1891 Nagant Rifle manufactured in 1924.

Nagant Rifle Model 91/30. Manufactured in 1936.

1940 Nagant Carbine.

Tokarev Rifle Model 1940. This semi-automatic rifle was manufactured in 1941.

Tokarev Rifle Model 1940 with ten round detachable magazine.

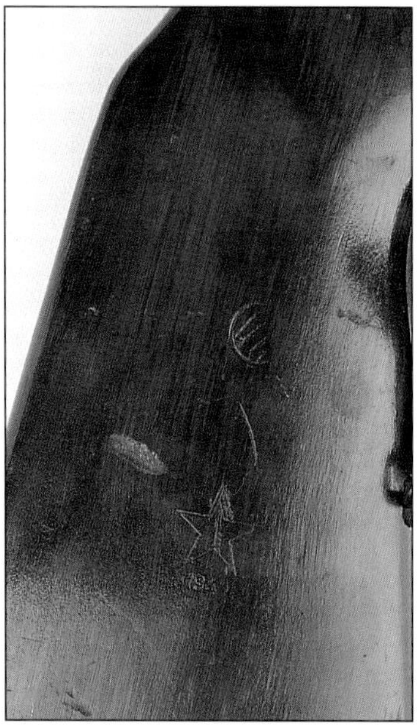

Tokarev stock markings showing logo for Tula Arsenal and the production date.

Opposite side of stock showing serial number on rifle.

The Model 1944 Nagant carbine is the same as earlier models with the exception of the bayonet. This model has a permanently mounted folding four cornered blade.

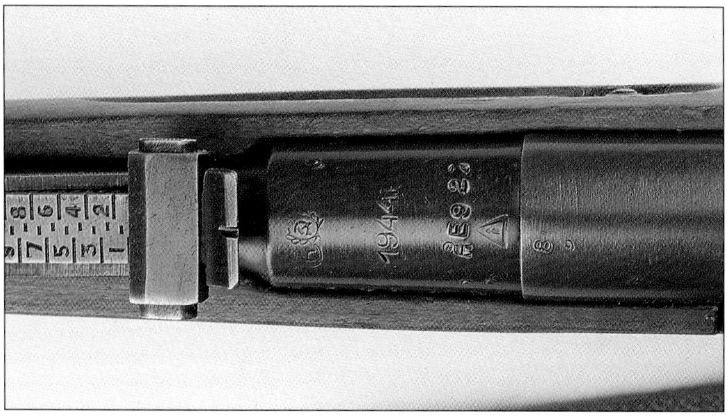

Nagant Sniper rifle dated 1944.

Detail of the detachable scope.

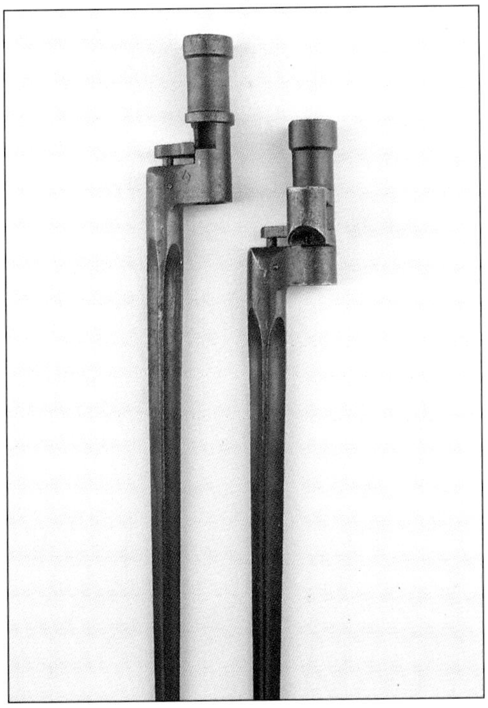

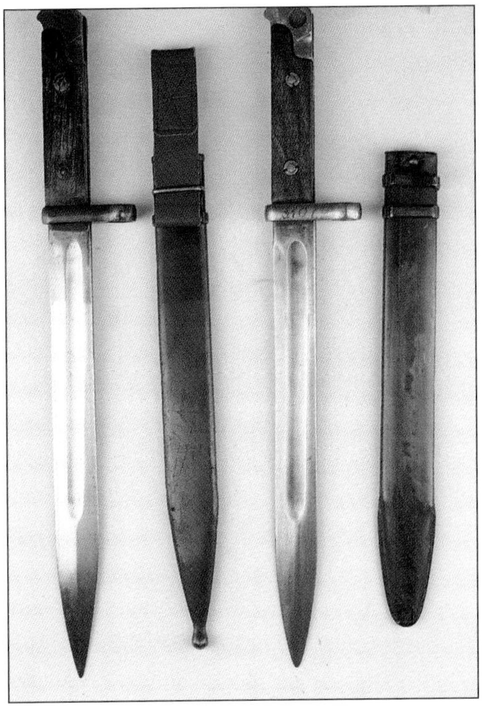

Left: Nagant Bayonets. The bayonet on the left is standard and the bayonet on the right has a built in sight hood that gives protection to the sight and when in use the sight picture is that of the 91/30. Center: Tokarev Rifle Bayonets. Pictured on the left is the last pattern bayonet produced. The scabbard end was simplified in its manufacture. The bayonet on the right was the first pattern bayonet used for the Model 1940 Tokarev rifle. Right: Opposite view of the Tokarev bayonets.

Above and below: Patriotic Post Cards.

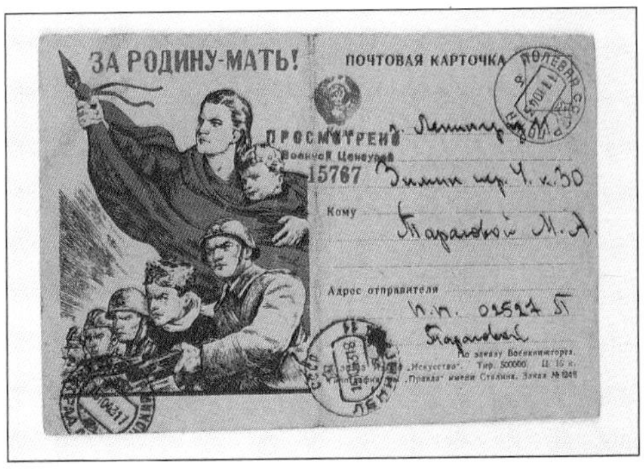

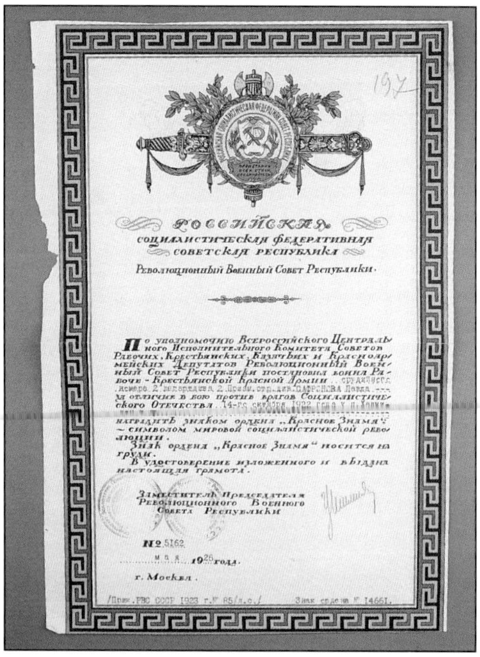

Document for Red Banner 1920s.

Border Guard proficiency document.

Savings bank circa 1930.

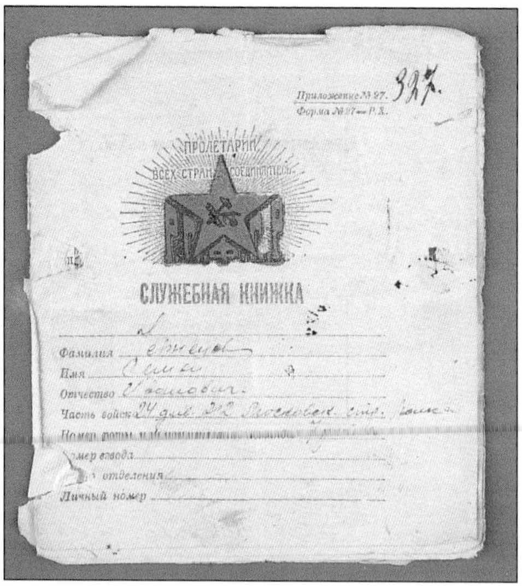

Identity document with the first pattern Star with Hammer and Plow.

Above and below: At first documents for Orders and Decorations were given out individually. Later a single book was used with new awards being added as they were earned. The first examples shown here are the Individual award books for a tank officer. One is for the twenty year jubilee of the Red Army or twenty year service in the Red Army. The second document is for battle action of "Akazan" against Japan in 1938.

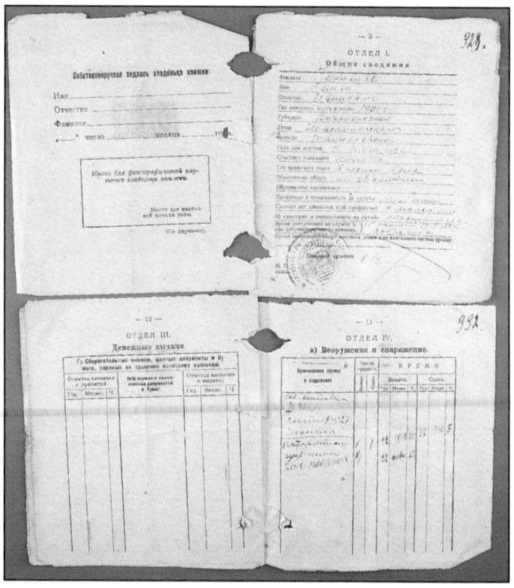

Inside of identity document.

Common style of flag pole top.

Tea cup from training school.

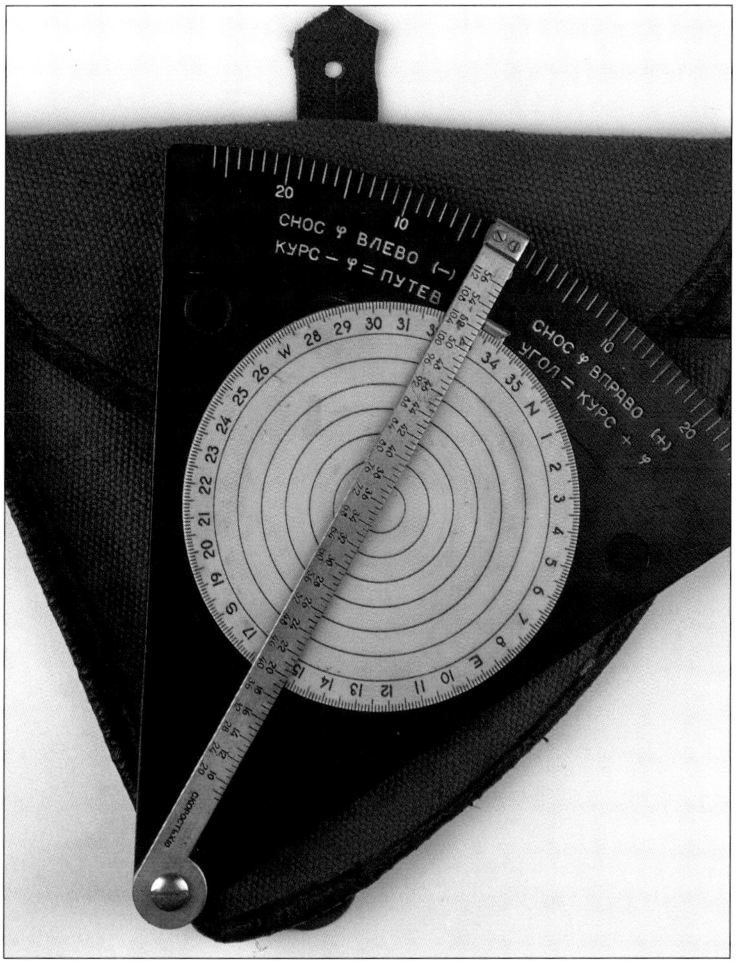

Left: Plotting instrument dated 1941.

Barometer dated 1941.

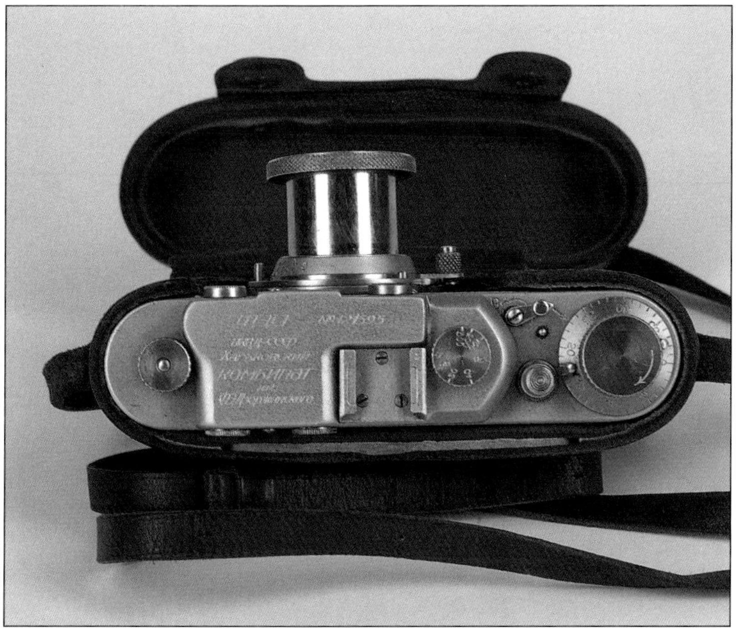

35mm camera made by FED. This is a direct copy of the Leica camera of the period. FED Company was run by the NKVD using orphan labor. The orphans were children of citizens deported or executed during the purges. The monogram of the NKVD is on camera body.

Classroom instruction on how to handle the fascist invader

Model 1936 helmet with red skeletal star. Also note the sight hood bayonet.

A well equipped sailor during the defense of Sevastopol.

All felt boots in use, 1942.

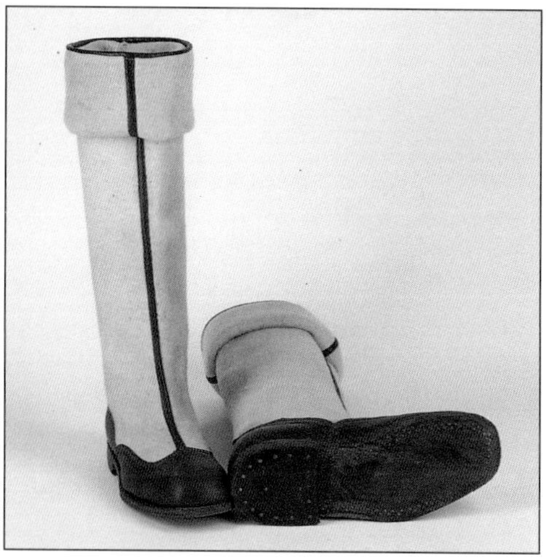

Felt Boots circa 1940. This was a style favored by some general officers.

Bibliography

Imperial General Staff. *Red Army Uniforms and Insignia, 1944.* London, UK. Arms and Armor Press. 1968.

Kharitonov, OV. *Soviet Military Uniforms and Insignia 1918-1958.* St. Petersburg Russia. Alga Fund Publishing Dept. of Alga Association and Neva Service. 1993.

Khvostov, Mikhail and Karachtchouk, Andrei. *The Russian Civil War (1) The Red Army.* London, UK. Osprey, an Imprint of Reed Consumer Book, Ltd. 1996.

Rosignoli, Guido. *Army Badges and Insignia of World War II.* New York, Macmillan Publishing Co Inc. 1972.

Seaton, Albert and Roffe, Michael. *The Soviet Army,* London, UK Hippocrene Books, 1972.

Shalito, Anton; Savchenkov, Ilya and Mollo, Andrew. *Red Army Uniforms of World War II.* London, UK. Windrow and Green Ltd. 1993.

Tokar, Leonid. *History of Russian Uniform: Soviet Police 1918-1991.* St.Petersburg, Russia. Exclusive Publishing House. 1995.

Zaloga, Steven and Volstad, Ron. *The Red Army of the Great Patriotic War 1941-5.* London, UK. Osprey Publishing Ltd. 1989.

Attractive display of militaria is important for every collector. Display products such as heads, torso forms, half mannequins, and full mannequins are available at reasonable costs. If you would like information on these products for your own display, send a large self addressed stamped envelope to the author: Dave Webster, P.O. Box 423, Albion, MI 49224.